MACHINE LEARNING WITH PYTHON:

DISCOVER HOW TO LEARN THE FUNDAMENTALS TO CREATE MACHINE LEARNING'S ALGORITHMS AND USE SCIKIT-LEARN WITH PYTHON EVEN YOU ARE A BEGINNER.

Table of Contents

Introduction

Machine learning originated from pattern recognition and the theory that computers are able to learn without the need for programming them to perform tasks. Researchers in the field of artificial intelligence wanted to determine whether computers are able to learn from data. Machine learning is an iterative approach, and this is why models are able to adapt as they are being exposed to new data. Models learn from their previous computations so as to give repeatable, reliable results and decisions.

Today, machine learning technology has given rise to sophisticated machines, which can study human behavior and activity in order to recognize fundamental patterns of human behavior and exactly predict which products and services consumer may be interested in. Under the side of their business model, businesses with an eye for the future gradually become technology firms with systems built upon machine learning algorithms. Consider some of the most innovative tech gadgets of this era such as "Amazon Alexa", "Apple's Siri" and "Google Home", what they all have in common is their underlying machine learning capabilities.

Because of the unique benefits of machine learning especially on the small devices, it is clearly becoming a favorite with businesses. From RPA functions to mobile automation it is all becoming a handheld reality bringing the future into the palm of your hands. Nowadays even the smaller businesses can leverage ML like the bigger boys. It can be used in cost-effective ways. For example, some companies use AI for improving customer relations. It reduces the costs and at the same time provides customized assistance to their companies. It can also be utilized to train the workforce and to improve forecasting cost-effectively. For example, Udacity which is an educational institution enhanced their sales by 50% by introducing chatbots to their sales teams. The advancements in data, algorithms and infrastructure and the costs required for getting them has decreased their overall costing and nowadays smaller businesses can afford them.

However, there are a host of questions raised about ethics in relation to machine learning. Systems that are trained on data sets with biases might lead to digitalization of cultural prejudices. For example, using data from a job hiring firm with racist policies will lead to machine learning systems duplicating the bias during the selection of applicants. Collecting "responsible data" and proper documentation of rules for algorithms to be used by systems has become significant. Even the languages contain biases and ML will have to learn them. Healthcare professionals developing the machines for generating income rather than serving people is another concern. There are some shining advantages as well. As AI will increase productivity in many jobs although lower and middle-level positions will get eliminated. In its position, several new positions with highly skilled, medium skilled and even low skilled range of people will be required.

Chapter 1: Jars of Machine Learning

The following components encompass the process of getting input and offering output, and they are;

- Learning

- Loss

- Task

- Data

- Evaluation

- Model

Learning

The responsibility of minimizing the error is the function of this algorithm. The algorithm defines the manner the variables in the equation are given value, so the output computed is close to actual production. For example:

In $y = mx+c$, the learning algorithm finds the values of m and c so that y) computed) is close to y (actual).

Loss

The difference between the actual output value and the output value that our model predicts or the rate of the error is the function of the loss. Minimizing the function of loss is quite vital for us to solve a problem.

Task

The thing we must do with the given data is what the task specifies for us. Task depends on the questions one has to solve with the available information. For example, based on the data, you can design a task to measure the happiness level of the employee or the performance of the employee.

Data

The fuel of machine learning is data, and you must learn to provide a proper history of data on the output and input. For example, an HR needs to give provision of all the employee information to have a prediction on whether or not an employee stayed or left or will leave the company.

Evaluation

We need to see the accuracy of the model to resolve the problem that we aim it to solve by identifying how well our model performs.

Accuracy = number of correct predictions/total number of predictions

When you test with some parts data, you can identify the precision that we gathered initially but make no use of it to train the model.

Model

The machine generates a formula that maps output and input or a model based on the data and input we provide. Where (x) is input and (y) is the output, a model can be like anyone of these equations;

There are three types of machine learning algorithms
1. Supervised learning

2. Unsupervised learning

3. Reinforcement learning

Supervised learning

For us to have an in-depth understanding of a supervised learning algorithm, we may first need to be familiar with the term "learning," since, as humans, we learn from our experiences. Therefore, when we tend to know the manner with which machine experience something, we will discover the extraordinary thing that machine data is the experience for them. Thus, as well as learning from the data which we learn from training data, learning from the data is the role of the algorithm of machine learning or any learning model. The things a supervised machine learning algorithm is attempting to do will be much more precise in mathematical terms.

For example, also known as one dimensional function, one variable, (that is, the x here) is $f(x) = x$. Likewise, two dimensional function example (two variables are x and y) is $f(x,y) = x + y$, and n-dimensional function example is $f(x1, x2.........., xN)$.

Types of functions are as follows:

Linear function:

When the graph of the function graph is a straight line, then we have linear function. We have linear function when any x1, x2..............., xN, the exponent of variables is comes to be 0 or 1. $f(x,y) = x+y+1$, $f(x) = x+1$, $f(x) =2$ are a few examples of the linear functions.

As you will see, the function of the graph below is linear since it has a straight line and it is the graph for $f(x) = x+1$.

f(x)=x+1 graph

Non-Linear function:

When the function graph is not a straight line, then we have the non-linear function. Also known as non-linear function, the exponents of the variables in the function are older than 0 or 1. Some examples of the non-linear function are $f(x) = x3$, $f(x) = x2$. The graph below is not a straight line and therefore, is for $f(x)=x^2$, showing the non-linear function.

Graph for $f(x)=x^2$

The attempt to identify this function $f(x1, x2........, xN)$ is what we are trying to do in supervised machine learning, where the features are x1, x2........, xN. Based on the data we are dealing with, this function could be anything linear or non-linear. To predict the output for us, when we obtain this function, then, we feed on the features. There are two types of supervised machine learning, depending on the output type.

Regression:

There is a regression problem when the output value is continuous. For example, we may call it regression since weight is a constant value when we are attempting to predict the weight of a person based on features like height.

Classification:

The classification problem is the process of the output value being discrete. For example, when a bank establishes the prediction of whether an individual is a fraud or not on specific features, then, the classification problem is this type of problem. Also, classifying the breed a dog belongs to is another excellent example of a classification problem.

Machine Learning Roadmap

Learning and revising the linear algebra is the right place to start. You will have a basic introduction to the entire core concepts of linear algebra. And take notice of matrix multiplication, vectors, Eigenvector decomposition, and determinants, as the whole lot of them contributes as the cogs that make machine learning algorithms work.

Your next focus should be calculus. Here, understanding and learning how to utilize derivatives for optimization and also their meaning must be your focal point.

These are tools of machine learning, and without them, you cannot get anywhere with machine learning.

Then, the next step is coding. Before utilizing the premade models in SciKit, you must learn to implement all algorithms from scratch in Python. Not only would you know how it works, but it would also give you an in-depth and better knowledge. While you may start anywhere you want, here are the following orders to follow for your algorithms:

- Linear Regression

- Logistic Regression

- Naive Bayes Classifier

- K – Nearest Neighbors (KNN)

- K – Means

- Support Vector Machine (SVM)

- Decision Trees

- Random Forests

- Gradient Boosting

Linear Regression

By fitting the observed data to a linear equation, linear regression is all about the effort to develop the correlation connecting two variables. To be an explanatory variable is the consideration for individual variable while a dependent variable is a consideration for the other. For example, you can use a model of linear regression to relate people's heights against their weights. In the initial stage, you must establish if at all, there is a connection between the interested variables before you try to fit in the linear model to observed data. It doesn't mean that single variable produces the other, that is, higher college grades don't cause higher SAT scores, except that the two variables have no significant connection. For determining the relationship strength between two variables, a helpful tool is a scatterplot. There may likely be any provision of a useful model while fitting a linear regression model to the data when there is no connection between the dependent variable and the projected descriptive, that is, there is no indication of any decreasing or increasing trends the scatterplot. The correlation coefficient is an indispensable numerical degree of connection between two variables, such that the correlation strength of the experimental data for both variables is a value connection -1 and 1. Where $\underline{Y}$ is, the dependent variable and $\underline{X}$ is the explanatory variables, an equation of the line of linear regression has the form $\underline{Y = A + BX}$. As the intercept (the value of $\underline{Y}$ when $\underline{X = 0}$), the slope of the line is $\underline{B}$ and $\underline{A}$.

Logistic Regression

As an extension of the linear regression model for classification problems and with two likely results, logistic regression models the probabilities for classification problems. Logistic regression is the solution for classification. To press a linear equation output between 0 and 1, it is the function of logistic rather than fitting a hyper-plane or straight line that the logistic regression model uses. The definition of the logistic function is as follows:

$$\text{logistic}(\eta) = \frac{1}{1 + \exp(-\eta)}$$

As such, it comes across in this form;

The logistic function. Between 0 and 1 is the output number. It outputs 0.5 at 0 inputs

To logistic regression from linear regression is a straightforward step. Between the features and outcome, and in the linear regression model, we have modeled them with a linear equation.

$$\hat{y}(i)=\beta 0+\beta 1 x(i)1+\ldots+\beta p x(i)p$$

We have a preference for probabilities connecting 0 and 1 for classification, and into the logistic function do we wrap the right side of the equation. Doing this will force the output to guess just values connecting 0 and 1.

Naive Bayes Classifier

Naïve Bayes is a straightforward machine learning classifier that is commonly-used yet effective. With the use of the Maximum A Posteriori decision rule in a Bayesian setting, Naïve Bayes is a probabilistic classifier that makes classifications. Also, it has its representation with the use of an elementary Bayesian network. The classifiers of Naïve Bayes are a traditional solution for problems like spam decision and have been particularly famous for text classification.

The model

With the features, x_0 through x_n and classes c_0 through c_k, the goal of any probabilistic classifier is not only to return the most likely type, but also to determine the probability of the features happening in each category. Consequently, we may wish to have the capacity to calculate $P(c_i / x_0, \ldots\ldots., x_n$ for each group. The Bayes rule is what we use to do this. Bayes rule has this feature;

It is likely to have a class c_i replacing A and B x_0 as our combination of features utilizing the framework of classification in x_n. $P9x_0,\ldots\ldots,$ x_n) may be normally hard for us to calculate with $P(B)$ as nomination, we can merely maintain the term $P(c_i / x_0,\ldots\ldots,x_n) \propto P(x_0,\ldots\ldots,$ $x_n / c_i) * P(c_i)$ instead of ignoring it, where calculating it can be quite easy when $\propto$ means "is propositional to" .$P(c_i)$; it may be more difficult to compute i.$P(x_0,\ldots\ldots, x_n / c_i)$ a class of the proportion of the data set. For computation simplification, we make the assumption that x_0 through x_n are conditionally independent given c_i, which gives us the power to say that $P(x_0,\ldots., x_n / c_i) = P(x_0 / c_i) * P(x_1 / c_i)$. Though the classifier nonetheless functions well in nearly all conditions, it acquires the term naïve Bayes classifier as the postulation is most liable not true. As a result, our final representation of class probability is the following;

When you calculate the individual $P(x_j / c_i)$ terms will depend on what distribution your features follow. Where the elements may be word counts, in the text of word classification, features may follow a multinomial distribution. In other cases, they may develop a Gaussian distribution where features are continuous.

K – Nearest Neighbors (KNN)

A simple algorithm that classifies the new case or data, based on the same measure, and stores all the available instances is K Nearest Neighbor. Based on how its neighbors are classified, it is mostly used to classify a data point. For example, wine with Myricetin and Rutime as the chemical components. Let's take the consideration of measurement of Myricetin vs. Rutime level with two data points, White and Red wines. Founded on how much Myricetin and how much Rutime chemical substance presents in the wines, the two of them have been analyzed and then fall on that graph.

Integrated into the mainstream of the process of voting, 'k' is a stricture that submits to the nearest neighbors' number in KNN. Also, it is wise to know whether the new wince is white or red if we assume to add a fresh glass of wine in the dataset.

In this situation, we are required to find out what the neighbors are. We can assume that k = 5 to achieve that. Then, the manner of the classification of the new data and with the greater part of votes from its five neighbors, red is the neighbor four out of five neighbors, red would be the classification of the new point.

K – Means

Without any target labels, K-means is an unsupervised learning algorithm that gives the ability to identify the same groups or clusters of data points within your data. Where assignment to the clusters is based on some distance or similarity measure to a centroid by grouping the data into K clusters is the issue with K means. Now, how do we solve this issue? It is okay if we could outline the steps involved.

1. To its nearest centroid is where each data point is assigned when we initiate the K starting centroids, and this process is what we can do randomly.

2. Attached to the respective cluster, we compute the centroids as the mean of the data points.

3. Pending the moment we can induce our stopping criteria, steps 1 and 2 is what we will do.

To be more precise, it is for squared Euclidean distance or Euclidean distance that we are attempting to optimize for in case you are wondering what is happening. To the cluster that minimizes this squared distance or groups closest to them is where they assign the data points.

For each data point to its assigned cluster, J is simply the sum of squared distances. Where (x_n), the data point, is attached to the (k) cluster, and 0 otherwise, an indicator function, R is equal to 1.

Support Vector Machine (SVM)

As an algorithm of a supervised machine learning algorithm, they use support vector machine for regression or challenges in classification. But it is in classification problems that they mostly use it. We design an item of each data in this algorithm as a tip in the space of n-dimension, where the features number you have is n, with the value of an individual coordinate as the same as the value of each feature. Then, through obtaining the hyper-plane which differentiates both classes quite well enough, we perform classification.

Chapter 2: The RISE Algorithm

Its essence in shape very summed up taken of co NSIST in: Each example or casor is it a vector of attribute pairs - value, j together with the specification of the class to the what belongs the example; the attributes they can be if symbolic and / or numerical. Each rule is formada for a conjunction of background Y a class involved Every antecand-dente is a condition on a single attribute and exists to the sumo a antecedent by every attribute, that is, there may be attributes that do not formpart ofnone of the background of a ruler. The conditions on sim attributes bugs aretest of samedad of the shape ji vto □ , where ito is the attribute and jv is one of your values runc-cough. The conditions on numerical attributes they take the interval form permissible for d i-chos attributes, that is, two1, jji vvto , whereonejv Y twojv are two legal values of the attribute ito. A rule covers an example if the example satisfies all the terms of the ruler; a rule wins to an example yes is the rule mcloser to the example of according to distance metric that will be described later. RISE looks for "Good" rules partie NDOwhat spec í-to the general, starting with Own conju n-to of examples of training as the first Set of rules. Laugh taking every ruler Y find the example plus near of the mismto class, what the ruler do not he has c u-open (i.e. what is at a distance moh what zero of the ruler) and try generalize from Forma m í-encourage the rule to cover the example. The new rule is incorporates to the set of rules replacing the rule old, if the effect of the change (the inclusion of the ruler in the set) s o-about the global accuracy is positive in opposite case It is not incorporated into the set. The generalizations are one Algorithm exhibited in the dissertation"TO Unified A p-proach to Concept Learning"presin tada in option tograde of Doctor in Philosophy in information Y Sciences of the computing by Pedro Morais thin Sundays in the college of California Irving., EU Year 1997, Y abstracts presented by sor creator in 2004.

Also accept if not produce no effect in the precision global of the set of rules. East proc e-dimiento repiyou until for each rule the generalization attempt fails. In the worst case, do not he makes any generalize a-tion, and the end result is a neighbor classifier plus near what uses everyone the examples of co n-training together as copies. The classification of each exampleplo test real i-za finding the ruler plus close to the example, and assigning to the example the class of said rule. The precision (in English, accuracy) IS) Acc (RS, of a set of rules RS over a set of examples IS it defines as the tailstion of axis m-plos that the set of rules classifies correct a-mind. classify correctlye n-you a example when the rule closest to example has The same class that the example. As set of examples IS is forever set of training that remains implicit (is tell, the precision will be denoted by Acc (RS)). The precision he measure using the Logic method "leave one out": c when trying to classify to an axis m-plo, the ruler corresponding to example takes off of the set of rules, unless already cover to another example too. Each example memorizes your distance to rule more close Y the class assigned to bliss ruler, when he generalize to a ruler, single is necessary do correspond that one rule with everyone the axes m-plos, and check follow to some example that do not won before and what effect produces that. The examples wrong classified previously what now with the generalization of Rule are classified correct a-mind increase the accuracy of set of regales, and the examples classified previously entity of way run ecta that with the generalization, now they are poorly classified, decrease the accuracy of the conjunct of rules. If the first are more numerous what the last, the change in the precision of the co n-together of reglto is positive Y he you accept in the new rule set, the new general ruled. The measure of distance used is a combination of the distance Euclidean for the attributes number i-cos and, a simplified version of the metric of difference of values of Stanfill and Waltz. Be) C, and..., and, (and AND ETOtwo one an example with value iand for the i - th attribute and class.

The ARISE software ARISE that sand describe in details in It constitutes an implementation of a classification algorithm bas adoin RISE, what change the form to of try the missing values, what It allows also of the classification, the induction of rules Y what do not is impelled in the versions of the software available in the University . The software It was tried and evaluated of way ex i-people con the objective of check yes he got a proper implementation of the algorithmor laugh and if the change in the way of try the values ausen tes They maintain the strengths of the original algorithm. further sand tried the ef convenience of the algorithm or impland-lied and of the product (ARISE), comparing the results obtained by the W softwareEKA using the algorithms ID3, C4.5 Y Nge for a group of sets of workouts available in the r e-position of The universityversatility of California of To gocame (ICU) (R epository of machine learning databases. Dept of Information and Computer Science, Unive r-sity of California, Irvine, CA,), with address Web for free download :http://www.ics.uci.edu/~mlearn/MLRepository.html.

An alternative strategy to treatmente n-to of missing values for the algorithm Laugh At istudio quand drove to choice of RI SEas the algorithm to be implemented, it is detectedcted of righ now a limiting in I left hergives. In cases e x-we stretch the strategy RISE's original handle missing values of the attributes like values leg í-scams, can drive to a situation in the what he get rules imprecise and to avoid that situ a-ci ng an alternative strategy proposed in thecase of numerical attributes is widely described by various authors. In the bibliography is it so widely referenced various strategies for the treatment of numerical attributes with values absent, among others:

Remove the set of training the examples that have missing values.

Replace the value absent by the mode of the media of attribute values. •

Replace the value of the absent attribute for fashion or the half of the values of the attribute for the class more frequently. Other techniques with support in the distributions of probability of attribute values.

Note: In the case of the attributes symbolic absent n-tees, are applicable the techniques previous siempre May its symbolic nature allow it.

Calculation of the "mean" of symbolic attributes The method plus simple what appears in the bibliogr a-trust for determine the half of the you values of a symbolic attribute is select the value plus c o-bad of attribute, without however rigor, of that m a-nera we would be referring to fashion instead of the media of the attribute And various coi authorsnciden in which does not produce the best accuracy in the classification location]. Given that the mean for attributes Numeric is the value that minimizes the variance, we can extrapolate That idea for try with attribute or-symbolic cough Is natural follow the mismto strategy what with the attributes numeric, Y the half It constitutes a mand-central tendency did a ideal for the approach of the distribution of attribute values Yes, symbolic. To determine the distance between two values of a symbolic attribute, Sundays and other authors use the metrics:

$$(x \quad SVDM \sum_{c}^{c} \left(c^h \mid x^i \right) \quad P_P\left(c^h \mid x^j \right) \quad (3)$$

It coincides with other authors, which if the di stances among all The pairs of values of a symbolic attribute using, there will be a VA bout attribute that will result with the less distance to res-to in case of tie, he might select ale a-toriamente the valor of the attribution to minim hoist, and that value that minimizes distances, genuinely can be considered the "average" of the set of values. Formally, as described in: The media of a set of values symbolic he can define as the value m (a value of attribute) that minimiza the variance of the set, that is,

$$\left(\sum \quad m = \min \right) \quad (6)$$

Where J is the set of values of attribute yesm-bolic and v is a value of the set Jm will act c o-mo the best approach for the values of cor n-together J, so similar tohalfway for valpray numeric, m will be replaced by every value simb o-set J and the m value that minimizes the equation be Tomara comwave "Average" of conju n-to of symbolic values J. That valor m of the attribute simbolic obtained as "half", he can replace by every one of the v a-absent lords of the attribute and it is normal wait what have a effect equivalent to what he gets in the case of numerical attributes with

16

missing values. With it is obtained a set of trainI feel "normal" (without attributes missing), on which e x-wiping the same concepts as for attributes numeric missing, he you will get a mbest or alike precision in the classification what yes he will use the co n-Original training together. Is idea has in against what for the calculation of m he requires obtain the distance between all the p a-railings of values of the attributes symbolic, is dand-cir, the calculation of)(x ji x,SVDM, a quantity of times equal to the amount of variations with repeat i-tion of a set con a total of elements same to amount of values that it has the attribute, t o-I send two values at the same time. Being iTO the quantity of values different of the atr i-symbolic buto i, the calculation of A i 2 di sta n- cias (that is the amount of couples of values of attributes what he they can form where interest the order that occupy each element of the couple) and that amount of distances have to be calculated for each symbolic attribute of the set of enter a-while it has at least one missing value. Dice what)(x ji x,SVDM is a function of say s-tancia has what 0=x)d (x, Y with that he pue of avoid iTO times the calculation previous (the distance of a value to the same is zero) Y the quantity of say s-tanks for him symbolic attribute I know educate A i 2 -A i . It could be used also the fact that x)d(Y,=Y)d (x, and with it reduce further la cant i-dad of calculations, but, complicates the c logic calculation of the expression in parentheses in. An optiming for him calculation of the half of symbolic values After calculated the sum to of the distances of everyone the values of a attribute symbolic respect to the first his values, for the second value, it Iran Changing the others values of the attribute, my n-behind the accumulated an of the as distances That go getting be less what the sum of the gaves-tankers of everyone the values respect to the first v a-lor, yes he they travel everyone the values of the attribute, is on the roars he new sum of the distances, of everyone the attribute values with respect to the second one was less than the received was sum and in that case sand act a-lists the new one smaller sum of distances Y the value of the attribute for the which he got, in this case the be increase.

In case contrary, to penalties the sum accumulated of the distances leave of be less what the sum between and change to the third value of attribute, without necessity of run them all, I don't know update the smallest sum and proceed to calculate the cumulative sum of the distances of all the values regarding to the third value, and so on. Following is idea he reduce considerably the calculations, to a level that justifies the use of this proposal to weigh of the light increase in the weather of complej i-give of the algorithm, what in the worst case, in what the "half" be the latest of the values of the attribute, is quadratic with respect to the amount of values of the attribute with more cantity of distinct values and that has at least one missing value.

Potentials of ARISE

1. Be introduce a strategy alternative to the treatment of attributes with missing values, don-of he concludes with the Benefits what the new one e s-Generation strategy.
2. It adopted a strategy of decrease in the number of rules, that in and find out it, and does not decrease the accuracy in the classification. He chose by remove the rules what are absorbed by other rules. A rule absorbs or contains another when meets that, both rules are of the same class for all attributes, it is also fulfilled that:
Yes the attribute is symbolic: are equals their worth or nothing no this I presented the value of attribute in one or both rules
Yes the attribute is numeric: the extreme lower of the condition (the INF) is less or same what the of the other and the extreme or higher (the SUP) is older or same than that of the other. Yes the previous he meets for all the terms present at the rules, then said rule a b-sip or contain the other. Example:
A) Yes outlook = sunny Y 69 <= temperature <= 75 Y 70 <= humidity <= 70 Then and is
3. Be discovered the inaccuracies what provokes in the classification, the presence of multiple instances of a case in set of training, which it's generate mistakes conceptual disclosed in the Web and that will constitute object of analysis in futures work a-jos.
4. ARISE makes validations of the data of entry and provides facilities for the acquisition of the cases to classify and for creation Y edition of sets of training, suitable for non-specialist users
5. The export to several languages It helps the eventual creation of expert systems.

6. The results of ARISE with 3 of the algorithms plus cited internationally on 17 c together internationals of tests show what this he behaves best also to count with the advantages They motivated their choice.

The results of the experiments made allow affirm that at replace missing values by the stockings of the valpray of their cor-corresponding attributes he maintains the precision of the algorithi t-mo and the generation of inaccurate rules is avoided. Also applying the ideas of:

1. Don't eliminate rules that don't earn examples two the algorithm ID3 is applicable only to sets of workouts with discrete attributes, by so much is go favored in the tests, then, it was only possible try 3 of the 17 conjuncough.

2. Incorporate the strategy to eliminate las rules absorbed by others

3. Do not admit repeated instances of a mismo case ARISE preserve the like the algorithm base, the superiority over the algorithms used as counterpart representatives of state of art of the classification algorithms. The described software It is an easy tool of use by specialists of the Health what makes possible the application of Artificial Intelligence (AI) techniques in support of diagnosis doctor based on the Methics o-In addition, it allows to export to the language natural, and to the languages of Programming: C ++, Java, Y Prolog the rules of decision generated and this generates eventually useful knowledge. To materializer the goal is makes the execution of Projects what allow create conju n-cough of training extracted of data of pacie n-tes Cubans, or enrich the set of attributes that can be valued (give it a decimal value, nominal u ordinal) cas result of the interview and revision physical what the doctor perform to the patient, Y that allow a close diagnosis. The comparison of the diagnoses is immediate made on the basis to com analysis supplementary co n-Clients, with diagnoses "Virtual" made in base only to the interview and the reconomy what the doctor makes to the patient and about that base get sets of workouts insurance, oriented to what is aspired in this proposal.

Chapter 3: Convolutional Neural Networks

Convolutional Neural Networks are one of the most commonly used artificial neural networks due to their ability to process and classify images. These algorithms are used in a variety of fields where photo search and image recognition are required. They are also useful in digitizing text, language processing, and can also be used to graphically represent audio data. However, their main purpose is image recognition, and it's worth nothing that this is the ability that brought attention to deep learning. As a result, CNN algorithms are now being implemented in drones, AI-driven cars, robotics, medical science and much more. It's safe to say that convolutional neural networks have taken science and tech to a new level. A CNN processes visual data as tensors. If you don't already know, a tensor is a matrix of numbers with additional dimensions, and it is formed by an array nested inside an array and so on. When it comes to convolutional neural networks, we are working with 4D tensors. In order to make this explanation clearer, let's imagine we are looking at a picture. We can understand and determine the height and width of it with ease, but what about depth? In the case of images the depth refers to the encoded colors, in other words the red, green, and blue color channels (or layers).We use convolution to produce feature maps (maps of image details), and they exist in a 4th dimension. In this situation our picture is not a two dimensional object, but a four dimensional volume instead.

But what is convolution? In math we are referring to the measuring of how much two functions overlap each other when they pass over each other. It's also important to note that CNNs are registering different signals every time they pass a filter over an image. For instance, when we map the margins of the image we can picture these filters as horizontal, vertical, and diagonal lines that pass over it.

Keep in mind that convolutional networks don't process and analyze images the same way restricted Boltzmann machine algorithms do. CNNs learn image data bit by bit, in pieces, known as feature maps, while RBMs analyze whole images.

Another aspect that might help you gain a better understanding of convolutional neural networks is the fact that the design is inspired by the brain's visual cortex. This is what gives people the ability to process and analyze visual imagery. There are light detecting receptors that capture light data in visual field layers that overlap. This is partially the reason why these image recognition algorithms are so popular when working with artificial intelligence and machine learning.

Here are some examples of the real world use of the convolutional neural network. Sometimes theory is too dry to give you an idea of the real impact this neural net has in this field, but maybe some live examples will better illustrate its application.

The vastly popular social media platform Facebook is probably the most popular example of this. Facebook has created DeepFace, which is a facial recognition system that can identify human faces with great accuracy. Some sources even venture to report that this is achieved with 97% accuracy. Keep in mind that the FBI's own facial identification system is known to be approximately 85% accurate. Another intriguing program using a convolutional neural network is DeepDream, created by an engineer from Google. In this example, the neural net is used to enhance images by giving them a hallucinogenic look. The images are over processed through algorithmic pareidolia. Other large tech companies such as Microsoft and IBM have also developed intelligent software with the use of CNNs.

Understanding the Architecture

The topology of convolutional neural networks is similar to that of the multi-layer perceptron. It's an acyclic graph constructed with layers that contain few nodes, and each layer communicates with the next.

One of the most important differences worth mentioning here is that this type of neural net has identical neurons. In other words, we have identical parameter values, as well as weight values. This is something that makes CNNs extremely efficient, because there are fewer values that need computing. Another key difference is the nodes have limited communication. That means the note inputs are connected locally, only to neighboring nodes.

Layers

Then we have a filter composed of 4 parameters that is applied to the layer in order to create the feature map. The four filter parameters are known as hyper-parameters and they represent size, depth, stride, and zero-padding.

The size is determined by calculating the filter's surface area. Here you should keep in mind that the filter's size has an impact on the output. This means that we need to control the output precisely, so that we can have an efficient network. It's also worth mentioning that sizeable filters often overlap, however this can be used to our benefit because it can lead to an improved accuracy rate.

The filter depth is about how many nodes we have inside a layer, and how many of them connect in the same area around the input. Keep in mind that we are still discussing images, and when we're talking about depth we aren't referring to image content. If you ever worked with Photoshop or any other image editing or manipulating software, you probably already know about the color channels. They are needed to describe the content of the image, and neural network nodes are mapped for the purpose of perceiving the red, green, and blue color channels. This is why under most circumstances filter depth is set to 3. If we increase the filter parameter we can gain more data on the image and unmask other properties that are difficult to learn. However, if we set the depth to a low value, we gain weaker results.

The third filter parameter is the stride, and its value determines the space between the neurons. If we have a stride equal to 1 and we are working with an image, we are going to set each pixel as the center of the filter. This causes outputs to increase and a great deal of layer overlap. What we can do is increase the stride value to reduce the overlap, however keep in mind that the outputs will also be reduced in size. The way fine tuning is done in this case is by simply making a judgment call based on balancing accuracy and size. Under most circumstances, however, it's probably a good idea to stick to lower values.

The fourth and final filter parameter allows us to reduce a layer's output size. Zero-padding achieves this by setting the border values of the receptive fields to 0. In convolutional neural nets when we are talking about receptive fields, we refer to the input space that has an effect over any specific unit that is part of the network. As a word of warning, when you set the zero-padding, make sure that all the areas are still covered by the filter. Another big advantage of a proper zero-padding setup is the ability to adjust the inputs and outputs to have an identical size. Preparing the input and output layers to be equal in size is quite standard, because this enables us to efficiently adjust the depth and the stride parameters. If we didn't have any zero-padding, we would require a lot of effort to set up the parameters properly and improve network performance. The borders of a filter might even degrade if we didn't have the padding.

Now the question is, how do we calibrate all of these parameters when we set up the network? There's a simple formula for this. Here's what it looks like:

O represents the layer's output, W the image size, F the filter size, P the zero-padding, and S the stride. Keep in mind when applying the formula that the layer's output might not always be an integer value, and this can lead to various issues. Luckily, you can compensate by performing adjustments to the stride.

Now that you understand more about the convolutional network layers and their parameters, let's discuss what convolution actually is. Simply put, it is a mathematical operator, just like multiplication, and it is mostly used to break down complicated equations into a simpler form. In other words, the process results a third function after performing an operation on two set functions. This results in a new function that is actually a derivative of the 2 original functions.

When we are working with a convolutional neural network, we have the input as the first element. When we apply this process to an image, it is actually assigned in the width and height of the image. Here we will have 3 pixel matrices, as you're probably guessing, for each color channel. These matrix values will range from 0 to 255.

The second component is the convolutional kernel, which consists of one matrix composed of floats. These numbers provide a filter to the input matrix, and the output is a feature map. This filter goes over the input and writes the feature map. This is where we find the main advantage of the convolution process. There is no need for feature engineering. For now, you should know that a feature engineering process is extremely challenging and demanding.

Training

You will notice that convolutional network learning is extremely similar to the previous processes. For instance, MLPs are pre-trained with convolutional nets, and backpropagation is needed to process the gradient during the pre-training phase.

Now let's briefly discuss the main steps that are performed during the training. First, we need to compute the feature maps. This is achieved by computing each one as a sum of them all convolved with the weight kernel that coincides. This step is called the forward pass. In the second phase, we calculate the gradients by convolving the exchanged weight kernels with the gradients. This is the backward pass. In the process we also need to calculate the loss of kernels in order to adjust their weights.

Keep in mind that the training process is slow, and it will take some time even if you have high end hardware.

Connecting the Pieces

Now it's time to put everything together and learn what is the most efficient way of connecting all the elements together. To better illustrate the implementation of a convolutional net, we are going to take a real world example and pick it apart.

One of the most well-known convolutional nets is called "LeNet", which has been around since the 80s. It's best known for its performance when working with images and handwritten digits, and that is what we are mainly interested in. This network relies on alternating convolution, pooling layers, and an MLP. In case you are not aware, pooling layers are often placed between convolutional layers because it reduces the number of parameters and computation needed inside the network.

The layers are connected partially, but the MLP is entirely connected. Every layer is composed of channels that allow us to build powerful filters. The pooling layers are implemented for dimensionality reduction so that the output is equivalent to the input. We also have a fully connected layer to which all computations are communicated. Here's a diagram of a LeNet layer to give you a better idea of the architecture:

While this implementation is great for some applications, it is not an efficient solution for everything. In many cases, this architecture won't perform well enough when it comes to more challenging scenarios. Luckily there's another architectural version of the LeNet network, and that is GoogleLeNet.

Also known as Google's Inception network, this architecture was developed to handle challenging image data. What do we refer to as challenging? You know all those terrible quality pictures and videos shot with a phone in low lighting conditions and with a lot of noise? That's what this convolutional network is supposed to deal with. A lot of image data found on the internet contains a lot of clutter and noise, thus making it look extremely granular and hard to understand.

We are not going to dig deeper into these examples because that doesn't fit the focus of this book.

Chapter 4: Natural Language Processing

Natural Language Processing (NLP) is a widely used field within Artificial Intelligence which mainly involves the interactions between the human language and the computer. You can find its applications in a large variety of areas such as Sentiment analysis, Spam detecting, POS (Part-Of-Speech) Tagging, Text summarization, Language translation, Chatbots and so on.

1 How would you explain NLP to a layman? Why is it difficult to implement?

NLP stands for Natural Language Processing, the ability of a computer program to understand the human language. It is an extremely challenging field for obvious reasons. NLP requires a computer to understand what humans speak. But, human speech is very often not precise. Humans use slang, pronounce the words differently and can have context in their sentences which is very hard for a computer to process correctly.

2 What is the use of NLP in Machine Learning?

At present, NLP is based on Deep Learning. Deep Learning algorithms are a subset of Machine Learning, which need a large amount of data to learn high-level features from data on their own. NLP also works on the same approach and uses deep learning techniques to learn human language and improve upon itself.

3 What are the different steps in performing Text classification?

Text classification is a NLP task used to classify the text documents into one or more categories. Classifying whether an email is spam or not, analyzing a person's sentiments from his post, etc. are text classification problems.

A Text classification pipeline involves following steps in order:

A.   ***Text cleaning***
B.   Text annotation to create the features
C.   converting those features into actual predictors
D.   using the predictors to train the model
E.   fine-tune the model to improve its accuracy.

4 What do you understand by Keyword Normalization? Why is it needed?

Keyword normalization, also known as text normalization, is a crucial step in NLP. It is used to transform the keyword into its canonical form, which makes it easier for later processing. It removes stop words such as punctuation marks, words like "a", "an", "the" because these words generally do not carry any weight. After that, it converts the keywords into their standard forms which improves text matching.

For instance, reducing all words to lower cases, converting all tenses to simple present tense. So, if you have "decoration" in one document and "Decorated" in the other, then both of them would be indexed as "decorate". Now, you can easily apply a text matching algorithm on these documents and a query containing a keyword "decorates" would match with both of the documents. Keyword normalization is a very good means of reducing the dimensionality.

5 Tell me about Part-of-speech (POS) tagging.

Part-of-speech tagging is a process of marking the words in a given text as a part of speech such as noun, preposition, adjective, verb etc. It is an extremely challenging task because of its complexity and owing to the fact that the same word could represent a different part of speech in different sentences.

There are generally two techniques used to develop POS tagging algorithms. The first technique is stochastic, which assumes that each word is known and can have a finite set of tags which are learnt during training. And the second technique is rule-based tagging, which uses contextual information to tag each word.

6 Have you heard of the Dependency Parsing algorithm?

Dependency Parsing algorithm is a grammar-based text parsing technique which is used for detecting verb phrases, noun phrases, subject and object in the text. "Dependency" implies the relations between the words in a sentence. There are various methods to parse a sentence and analyze its grammatical structure. Some of the common methods include Shift-Reduce and Maximum Spanning Tree.

7 Explain Vector Space Model and its use.

Vector Space Model is an algebraic model which is used to represent an object as a vector of identifiers. Each object (such as a text document) is written as a vector of terms (words) present in it with their weights.
For instance, you have a document "d" with the text "This is an amazing book for the interview preparation."
The corresponding vector for this document is:

$$d = (w_{amazing}, w_{an}, w_{book}, w_{for}, w_{nterview}, w_{is}, w_{preparation}, w_{the}, w_{this})$$

There exist many ways to calculate these weights w_i. They can be as simple as just the frequency (count) of the words in a document. Similarly, any query is also written in the same fashion. And, the vector operations are used to compare the query with the documents to find the most relevant documents that satisfy the query.
Vector Space Model is used extensively in the fields of Information Retrieval and Indexing. It provides a structure to the unstructured datasets, thereby making it easier to interpret and analyze them.

8 What do you mean by Term Frequency and Inverse Document Frequency?

Term Frequency (tf) is the number of times a term occurs in a document divided by the total number of terms in that document.

Inverse Document frequency (idf) is a measure of how relevant is the term across all the documents. Mathematically, it is the logarithmic of (total number of documents divided by the number of documents containing the term).

9 Explain cosine similarity in a simple way.

Cosine similarity captures the similarity between two vectors. As explained in the vector space model, each document and the query is written as a vector of terms.

The cosine is calculated for the query vector with each document, which is normal cosine between two vectors. The resulting cosine value represents the similarity of the document with the given query. If the cosine value is 0 then there is no similarity at all and if it is 1, then the document is the same as the query.

10 Explain N-gram method.

Simply put, an N-gram is a contiguous sequence of n items in the given text. N-gram method is a probabilistic model used to predict an item in a sequence based on the previous n-1 items. You can choose the items to be either the words, phrases etc. If n is 1, then it is called 1-gram, for n = 2, it is 2-gram or bigram and so on.

N-grams can be used for approximate matching. Since they convert the sequence of items into a set of n-grams, you can compare one sequence with another by measuring the percentage of common n-grams in both of them.

11 How many 3-grams can be generated from this sentence "I love New York style pizza"?

Breaking the given sentence into 3-grams, you get:

A.   ***I love New***

B.   ***love New York***

C.   ***New York style***

D.   **York style pizza**

We will use CountVectorizer package to demonstrate how to use N-Gram with Scikit-Learn.

CountVectorizer converts a collection of text documents to a matrix of token counts.

In our case, there is only one document.

```
from sklearn.feature_extraction.text import CountVectorizer
```

N-gram_range specifies the lower and upper boundary on the range of N-gram tokens

to be extracted. For our example, the range is from 3 to 3.

We have to specify the token_pattern because, by default, CountVectorizer treats single character words as stop words.

```
vectorizer = CountVectorizer(ngram_range=(3, 3),
                 token_pattern = r"(?u)\b\w+\b",
                 lowercase=False)
```

Now, let's fit the model with our input text

```
vectorizer.fit(["I love New York style pizza"])
```

This will populate vectorizer's vocabulary_ dictionary with the tokens.

Let's see the results of this vocabulary

```
print(vectorizer.vocabulary_.keys())
```

12 Have you heard of the Bag-of-Words model?

The Bag-of-Words model is a very common technique used in Information Retrieval and Natural Language Processing. It is also known as the Vector Space Model, which is described in detail in question 6 above. It uses the frequency of occurrence of the words in a document as the feature value.

One of the limitations of this method is that it does not take into account the order of the words in a document due to which you can not infer the context of the words. For instance, if you take these two sentences "Apple has become a trillion dollar company" and "You should eat apple every day", the Bag-of-Words model won't be able to differentiate between Apple as a company and Apple as a fruit. To address this limitation, you can use N-gram model which stores the spatial information of the words. Bag-of-Words is a special case of N-gram method with n=1.

Chapter 5: Logistic Regression

Machine learning models usually boil down to predicting a quantitative outcome or a qualitative class. The former is commonly referred to as a regression problem, and in the case of linear regression this involves predicting a numeric outcome based on the input of continuous variables. In the case of predicting a qualitative outcome (class), the task is considered a classification problem. Examples of classification problems include predicting what product a user is likely to buy or predicting if a target user will click on an online advertisement (Yes/No).

Not all algorithms, though, fit cleanly into this simple dichotomy and logistic regression is a clear example. Logistic regression is part of the regression family, because as with linear regression, it involves predicting outcomes based on analyzing quantitative relationships between variables. But unlike linear regression, it accepts both continuous and discrete variables as input and its output is qualitative; it predicts a discrete class such as Yes/No or Customer/Non-customer.

Logistic regression analyzes relationships between variables and assigns probabilities to discrete outcomes using the Sigmoid function, which converts numerical results into an expression of probability between 0 and 1.0.

A value of 0 represents no chance of occurring, whereas 1 represents a certain chance of occurring. For binary predictions, we can assign two discrete classes with a cut-off point at 0.5. Anything above 0.5 is classified as class A and anything below 0.5 is classified as class B.

A sigmoid function used to classify data points

After assigning data points to a given class using the Sigmoid function, a hyperplane is used as a decision boundary to split the two classes to the best of its ability. The decision boundary can then be used to predict the class of future data points.

Logistic regression hyperplane is used to split the two classes

Logistic regression can also be used to classify multiple outcomes but is generally used for binary classification (predicting one of two discrete classes). Other techniques, including the Naive Bayes classifier and support vector machines (SVM), are considered more effective at classifying multiple discrete outcomes.

Exercise

This exercise uses logistic regression to predict the outcome of a Kickstarter campaign, and specifically, whether the campaign will reach its target funding in the form of a binary "0" (No) or "1" (Yes) outcome. Kickstarter.com is an online crowd-funding platform for creative projects and new products.

1) Import libraries

The libraries used for this exercise are Pandas, Seaborn, Matplotlib and Pyplot (a MATLAB-like plotting framework that combines Pyplot with NumPy), as well as Scikit-learn.

```
import pandas as pd

import matplotlib.pyplot as plt

import seaborn as sns

%matplotlib inline

from sklearn.model_selection import train_test_split

from sklearn.linear_model import LogisticRegression

from sklearn.metrics import confusion_matrix, classification_report
```

2) Import dataset

The next important step is to import the CSV dataset into Jupyter Notebook as a Pandas dataframe.

```
df = pd.read_csv('~/Downloads/18k_Projects.csv')
```

Kickstarter Projects dataset

3) Remove variables

Step three is to remove non-essential variables using the delete method.

```
del df ['Id']

del df ['Name']
```

```
del df ['Url']

del df ['Location']

del df ['Pledged']

del df ['Creator']

del df ['Category']

del df ['Updates']

del df ['Start']

del df ['End']

del df ['Latitude']

del df ['Longitude']

del df ['Start Timestamp (UTC)']

del df ['End Timestamp (UTC)']

del df ['Creator Bio']

del df ['Creator Website']
```

We have removed 16 variables from the dataframe. Some variables were removed because they are strings or timestamps which cannot be parsed and interpreted as numeric values by logistic regression. Not all non-numeric variables were removed, as we will transform some of these variables using one-hot encoding in Step 4.

4) Convert non-numeric values

Logistic regression accepts discrete variables as input provided they are expressed numerically. Consequently, we need to convert the remaining categorical features into numeric values using one-hot encoding.

```
df = pd.get_dummies(df, columns=['State', 'Currency', 'Top Category', 'Facebook Connected', 'Has Video'])
```

Finally, let's inspect the shape of the dataframe for future reference.
```
df.shape
```

Run the model.

OUTPUT: (18142, 36)

The dataframe has 18,142 rows and 36 columns/features.

5) Remove and fill missing values

Let's now inspect the dataframe for missing values.

df.isnull().sum()

Run the model.

Comments	0	Currency_NZD	0
Rewards	0	Currency_USD	0
Goal	0	Top Category_Comics	0
Backers	0	Top Category_Crafts	0
Duration in Days	0	Top Category_Dance	0
Facebook Friends	5852	Top Category_Design	0
Facebook Shares	0	Top Category_Fashion	0
Creator - # Projects Created	0	Top Category_Film & Video	0
Creator - # Projects Backed	4244	Top Category_Food	0
# Videos	101	Top Category_Games	0
# Images	0	Top Category_Journalism	0
# Words (Description)	0	Top Category_Music	0
# Words (Risks and Challenges)	101	Top Category_Photography	0
# FAQs	0	Top Category_Publishing	0
State_successful	0	Top Category_Technology	0
Currency_CAD	0	Top Category_Theater	0
Currency_EUR	0	Facebook Connected_Yes	0
Currency_GBP	0	Has Video_Yes	0

The output shows that only four of the current 36 variables contain missing values.

#Code for obtaining correlation coefficients
df['State_successful'].corr(df['Facebook Friends'])
df['State_successful'].corr(df['Creator - # Projects Backed'])
df['State_successful'].corr(df['# Videos'])
df['State_successful'].corr(df['# Words (Risks and Challenges)'])

Summary of variables with missing values

The variables **Facebook Friends** and **Creator - # Projects Backed** have a high number of missing values but their correlation to the dependent variable (**State_successful**) is strong. Removing rows containing missing values from these two variables would also cut the dataset in half (from 18,142 rows to 9,532 rows).

Regarding the other two variables, we can remove the missing rows given their low frequency (101). Alternatively, you could opt to remove these two variables given their low correlation with the dependent variable.

Next, let's use the **describe()** method to inspect the standard deviation and range of the two remaining variables.

df.describe()

The standard deviation (std) and range (max – min) for the variable **Facebook Friends** are high but much lower for the variable **Creator - # Projects Backed**.

Let's take one final look at these variables using a distribution plot using Seaborn and Matplotlib/Pyplot.

#Distribution plot of variable 'Facebook Friends'

plt.figure(figsize=(12,6))

sns.distplot(df['Facebook Friends'], kde=True, hist=0)

#Distribution plot of variable 'Creator - # Projects Backed'

plt.figure(figsize=(12,6))

sns.distplot(df['Creator - # Projects Backed'], kde=True, hist=0)

Owing to high variance, it appears unreasonable to fill the variable Facebook Friends with the mean, mode, or another artificial value, as none of these methods provides a reliable fill value. Also, due to the significant correlation of this variable to the dependent variable, we don't necessarily want to remove it from the model. We'll therefore proceed by retaining this variable and removing rows with missing values.

We have a similar problem with the variable Creator - # Projects Backed, but due to its lower range, standard deviation, and correlation to the dependent variable, we can fill this variable with the mean without significantly altering patterns in the data.

```
# Fill missing values for 'Creator - # Projects Backed' with the
mean value
df['Creator - # Projects Backed'].fillna(df['Creator - # Projects
Backed'].mean(), inplace=True)
```
Drop remaining missing values for remaining variables

df.dropna(axis=0, how='any', thresh=None, subset=None, inplace=True)

df.shape

Run the model.

OUTPUT: (12215, 36)

Following these alterations, we have 12,215 rows, equivalent to two-thirds of the original dataset.

6) Set X and y variables

The dependent variable (y) for this model is the binary variable State_successful, This means we can remove the variable State_failed because it won't be used as an input (X) or output (y) variable.

del df ['State_failed']

The remaining variables are the independent variables (X). Rather than calling each variable in the code separately as performed in the previous exercise, we can call the full dataframe and remove the y variable using the drop method.

X = df.drop('State_successful',axis=1)

y = df['State_successful']

Shuffle and split data 70/30.

X_train, X_test, y_train, y_test = train_test_split(X, y, test_size=0.3, random_state=10, shuffle=True)

7) Set algorithm

Assign **LogisticRegression()** to the variable **model** or a variable name of your choosing.

model = LogisticRegression()

Fit the algorithm to the training data.

model.fit(X_train, y_train)

8) Evaluate

Using the predict function on the X_test data, let's compare the predicted results with the actual outcome of the y_test set using a confusion matrix and classification report from Scikit-learn.

model_predict = model.predict(X_test)

#Confusion matrix

print(confusion_matrix(y_test, model_predict))

#Classification report

print(classification_report(y_test, model_predict))

The confusion matrix indicates that we had 171 false-positive predictions and 211 false-negative predictions. The performance of the model, though, is put into perspective when considering the strong precision, recall, and f1-score conveyed in the classification report.

8) Predict

Let's now use our model to predict the likely outcome of an individual Kickstarter campaign based on the input of its independent variables.

new_project = [

0, #Comments

9, #Rewards

2500, #Goal

157, #Backers

31, #Duration in Days

319, #Facebook Friends

110, #Facebook Shares

1, #Creator - # Projects Created

0, #Creator - # Projects Backed

0, ## Videos

12, ## Images

872, ## Words (Description)

65, ## Words (Risks and Challenges)

0, ## FAQs

0, #Currency_AUD

1, #Currency_CAD

0, #Currency_EUR

0, #Currency_GBP

0, #Currency_NZD

0, #Currency_USD

0, #Top Category_Art

0, #Top Category_Comics

0, #Top Category_Crafts

0, #Top Category_Dance

0, #Top Category_Design

0, #Top Category_Fashion

1, #Top Category_Film & Video

0, #Top Category_Food

0, #Top Category_Games

0, #Top Category_Journalism

0, #Top Category_Music

0, #Top Category_Photography

0, #Top Category_Publishing

0, #Top Category_Technology

0, #Top Category_Theater

0, #Facebook Connected_No

0, #Facebook Connected_Yes

0, #Has Video_No

1, #Has Video_Yes

]

Chapter 6: Django And Web Application

In fact, pretty much all business segments have started to use machine learning at some point or another. Machine learning has been able to take a role in our daily lives, and it is slowly but surely starting to represent something that is pretty well-known and concrete in the minds of the public.

However, just because it is more recent and is just starting to grow, don't be fooled into thinking that it is going to be a cutting-edge option or it is only for businesses that have a ton of money to keep up with the latest and greatest in the technology. In fact, machine learning and some of the techniques that come with it have been around for some time, and you will find that ignoring machine learning can be a bad thing for your business.

Think of it this way, do you see it as a waste of the time of your employees to work on a task that could be automated and done for them? Is it a waste of your valuable data when it just sits in a database, waiting for someone to have the time and resources to get to it? Or do you feel that it is a waste of the final product when it is delivered without being able to reach the full capacity of what it should be able to do? If you answered yes to any, but most likely all, of these questions, then machine learning is something that you need to spend some time on.

But here comes the next question, how are you able to implement machine learning in business, implanting it as a tool for your engineers or as a service for your clients? How do you streamline it without having to have experts in the field handle it all of the time? That is what we are going to explore in this chapter!

Working with an API in machine learning

Offering a machine learning solution with the help of this API is going to allow a person to focus more on the results, while still ensuring that the developers you have working on machine learning have full control to maintain the model that comes with it.

Using the API is going to prove itself as an efficient way of delivering machine learning. This is true even with companies who have large AI divisions and who will really apply this in an extensive manner, such as what we see with Google and Amazon.

Now we need to go back to the idea of some of the advances that come with Machine learning. Another factor that we need to consider for its role in why this method is being adopted so well is because of the exceptional libraries that come with Python. Python is one of the best languages to use with machine learning because of all that you are able to do with it, and you will find the libraries are going to be even better. In particular, you will find that some of the libraries like TensorFlow, pandas, and scikit-learn are going to make it so much easier for your developers to come up with solutions that are high quality in machine learning.

You can easily see why the Python language is going to be the most used programming language in data science and machine learning. Nothing else even comes close! The language is not only simple enough for a beginner to use and learn, but it is also going to have the power and functionality to handle some of the more complex tasks that you are going to do in machine learning.

One thing that we need to take a look at here is the idea of Django from Python. Django is really easy to get started with, it has the stability that you need, and it is already integrated with the libraries that come with Python, so you won't have to worry about that.

The Django web framework was first developed because there were several developers of a newspaper's online site who were tired of the type of framework that they were using at the time. They wanted to be able to work with a Python version and use it to build up the backend that was needed of the portal. Because of this need, Django was developed.

Since it was first developed, Django has seen a lot of success, mainly form its ease of use. You will find that over time, it has grown to become one of the top four web frameworks that are being used on many businesses and websites. In fact, some major websites like Disqus and Instagram are already using this framework to keep themselves up and running.

Plus, this framework is going to be able to help you out with a lot of the major issues and questions that you run into when it is time to implement machine learning and the Python language online. Adding to the Django REST Framework and a web server of your choices (working with Guincorn is a great option if you are looking for one), it is possible for you to get a Python-based API up and running in no time, allowing you to work with the solution that you need with machine learning.

More about Django

Let's take a closer look at some of the things you should know about Django and how to use it. Django is a framework that was written out in Python. A framework is just going to be a collection of modules that are brought together in a manner that makes development easier on those who are using it. These are going to be put in a program together and this allows you to create a website or another application using an existing source, rather than having to start straight from nothing each time.

This is how many websites, even those that are developed at home by one person, are able to include some more advanced features and functionality, including contact forms, file upload support, management, and admin panels, comment boxes and more. Whether you want to create a web application for yourself or for a business, you will find that using a framework like Django could give you a high-quality product without having to be a programmer on your own. By using the Django framework, the components that you need for this are going to be in there already, you just have to take the time to configure them in the proper manner to match your site.

When we take a look at the official site for Django, it is basically a high-level web framework from Python that is going to encourage the rapid development of a project, along with a design that is pragmatic and clean. This framework, even though it is open sourced, was built up by developers experienced in Python, and it takes care of a lot of the hassle that comes with web development. This allows a lot of people to work on this framework, even if they have no web development experience to go from.

When we use a framework like Django or some of the other ones, it makes life easier. The framework is going to take care of the web development part so that you are able to focus on writing your app, without having to reinvent the wheel and start from the beginning each time. plus, Django is open sourced and free, making it the perfect choice for those who want to create their own website and those who need to do it for a company or business.

Django is going to be a great option to use because it offers us a big collection of modules that you are able to use with any of the web-based projects you want to focus with. Mainly though, the Django framework was designed in order to save wasted time for developers and to make life easier.

Another thing that you may find interesting when it comes to Django is that it was created with the idea that front end developers would be the ones most likely to use it. The template language is going to be designed in a way to make you feel comfortable, and it is going to be easy for anyone to learn in order to work with HTML, including front end developers and designers. But it is also going to be easily extensible and flexible, allowing developers to augment the template language as needed.

If you do plan to do some work with machine learning and Python, especially if you are trying to do this with web design and web applications, it is a good idea to bring in the Django framework to help you out. There are a lot of different ways that you can use, and it is going to make your life easier.

How to get started with Django

Now that we understand a bit more about Django and what it is all about, it is time to move on to a few of the other things that you are able to do with this program. Django is going to adhere to what is known as the MVT architectural pattern, or model view template. After you have taken the time to install it and you have all of the necessary information and files in place for it, you will need to get to executing it. The command that is needed to do this includes:

Django-admin startproject mysite

When you work with this command, it is going to create most of the configurations and structure that you need for that folder to get the project up and running. Once you have given that command some time to get up and running, it is time to get yourself into the folder for the project. Any time that you want to do this, work with the following code:

Python manage.py startapp myapp

At this point, you have created the app that is going to be able to run the correct machine learning API that you need. Next, you need to take some time to edit out the models/py of the app, that is, if you plan to use a database to go along with this project. And don't forget to take some time to create what is known as the API Views to make this all work together well.

47

For the most part, you will find that your machine learning model is going to be accessed from this API Views when you need it. This means you just need to add the views.py file to the mix to get it. One of the methods that you can use to make the integration of the model and the server happen is that, when you are done building and then validating the model to make sure it works, you will save up any of the binaries that come up with Pickle. From there, you can add all of these codes into a package, and then import them over to the View.

In addition to this, there are times when you may find the model is going to be too large for the storage you have, or it may be too large for other reasons. If this is true of your file, then it is a good idea to load this in a new way, as a global variable in this file. This ensures that the file is only going to load one time. Traditionally, this is going to load up every time that you try to call up the view. When the file is large, this is going to slow down the computer and can even cause things to get stuck. But with the steps that we just did, we are basically asking it to just load up once, any time that you start up the server, rather than each time you start up the View.

As you can see here, there are a lot of great features that you are able to use when it comes to Django. It is a fast and reliable way for you to take some of your machine learning models and get them to work for you. And it works in Python which can make things even easier for you to work with. Taking the time to get it downloaded and making sure you get it set up with the right Python libraries will ensure that it is ready to handle any of the web-based models that you would like to do with your project.

Chapter 7: Developing Models

You will need to get yourself set up in Python or some other programming language to do machine learning. You create machine learning models by using code to manipulate the datasets. While this book doesn't cover coding for machine learning, I will give you a quick rundown of some basic libraries and packages that I recommend you install for machine learning.

Because it's the most common language used in data science, we will use Python as an example throughout this chapter. I also think it's the most practical language to learn if it's your first language because it's more readable than other programming languages, and it has a wide range of abilities beyond machine learning.

Once you've installed the latest version of Python, there are a few recommended libraries to install which come with a lot of commands that will be useful to your work with machine learning. All of these can be found easily with a quick google search, and they can be downloaded for free.

The most important library for data analysis and machine learning in Python is called Pandas. It's quite a popular choice for datasets and will make your coding easier and faster, especially when you are still trying to get a feel for things.

Anaconda for python

Another option for getting yourself started with Python is installing Anaconda. The great thing about Anaconda is that it gives you every package for Python so that you don't have to install packages one at a time while you write the program for your model. It comes with all the libraries you will need, for just about every different kind of function.

Anaconda is a free and open-source program that will work in both R and Python. With Anaconda, you'll have access to several libraries that will help you with your data science projects. Basically, this gives you a pre-packaged collection of all the python libraries, of which there are over 100 libraries.

One of the major libraries is Spyder and Jupyter. Both of these are integrated development environments, meaning they are the window where you will write your code, but they are more developed than a standard command window and have options to save and export/import codes.

Most Python users will start in a development environment called IDLE. It's very simple and offers a good format for learning how to code in python. When you install Python on a windows computer, it will come automatically included. If you have a Linux computer, it is available, but you will need to install it separately.

IDLE will make those baby steps in Python easier because you'll be able to save your scripts and edit them later. It will also walk you through debugging.

To install Anaconda, visit:

docs.anaconda.com/anaconda/install

Scroll down until you see a list of operating systems. Choose your operating system. It will give you instructions for installing anaconda on their website, based on your operating system. Then you're ready to start messing around in Python. I highly recommend using one of the free beginner Python tutorials that are available on the internet. EdX has a free beginner tutorial in Python, which is a great place to start. Also, take advantage of forums like Reddit, where there have been a vast number of common questions already answered in detail, and members are always sharing relevant news from the world of machine learning.

Algorithms

Once you have your data, and the hardware and software to manipulate it, you need to bring them together. Put your data on your programming software. Find a dataset for free online to work with when you are first starting out. Kaggle.com is free and has a lot of data sets to choose from in CSV format, which will be easy to work with once you have Pandas library imported into your Python.

The best algorithms to start with are linear and logistic regression for supervised learning and k-means clusters in unsupervised learning. These will be relatively easy starting out, and you can build towards other models from there.

Visualization tools

You have your data, and now you have created models using one of the programming languages, and you have a whole collection of data science libraries to help you do all this faster. Your computer is running well, and you can create models independently.

You may have created models that display interesting results, but in order to break it down into layman's terms and communicate your findings with stakeholders, you'll need to organize it in a way that's easy to visualize. If you're a data scientist on a marketing project, you may have created a model that helps break down customers into categories and predicts trends in buying habits. But if you want to communicate these results to the rest of your marketing team, you'll need to find a way to communicate so that even people who aren't familiar with data science can understand your results. Breaking down your data into charts and graphs and visual will help compliment your analytics skills. Being able to make visualizations of your data is extremely important when you are communicating with an audience who isn't familiar with data analysis

A popular toolset for data professionals is Tableau. Tools like these are called data visualization software. At some companies, there are employees whose entire job involves taking hard to read data and presenting it in a way that is easy to visualize.

Software like tableau is very commonly used by businesses that rely on data to make decisions. Tableau is useful because its relatively easy to use, and data can be viewed in real-time through its platform. You can customize a dashboard of tools for creating reports and charts with your data. It also gives you the ability to share your results with other people from your company. Tableau can be used to create graphs and scatterplots from that data that you have analyzed in your programming language.

More advanced things which are useful

These tools may not be as relevant to you when you are just beginning, but it might be interesting to talk about some of them and consider what may be useful down the road. This book may just the beginning on your path to be a machine learning expert, so you may refer to this list later when you are a little more advanced.

You should continue to think about the management of unstructured data. Usually, this requires more advanced programs because it is more difficult to manage and manipulate. This type of data often takes on the form of something much too complicated for the human brain to analyze without the assistance of tools, but this is the direction where machine learning is heading. Using neural networks to mimic the functions of human thought, who knows what the future will hold.

The further we get with machine learning, the bigger our data is getting. Possibilities of machine learning are expanding all the time. The data that is important in the future won't have the neat structure we are accustomed to, like the kind of data that can fit in an excel sheet.

This type of data also requires beefier computer hardware and software to be able to handle the processing of these large quantities of information. Usually use some sort of cloud computing software to carry the large volumes of information, as well as a GPU specific to data analytics. This higher level of computing can help to process multiple moving points at once. The math required also becomes harder. Combining algorithms.

Chapter 8: Data Pre-Processing and Creation of Training Data Set

Data Preprocessing is a "data mining technique, which is used to transform raw data into a comprehensible and effective format". Real-world data tend to lack certain behaviors or trends and is almost always incomplete, inconsistent and/or missing attribute values, flooded with errors or outliers. Preprocessing data is a proven way to solve such problems. This raw data or real data from the world cannot be readily transmitted through a machine learning model. Therefore, before feeding real-world data to a machine learning model, we need to clean and pre-process it.

Overview Data Preprocessing

Data Cleaning

Many meaningless and missing sections can be found in the data. "Data cleaning" is performed to manage these inadequacies and constitutes handling data set that is missing values and consists of noisy data.

Missing Data

In this scenario, certain significant information in the data set is missing. It can be dealt with in different respects such as:

Ignoring the tuples: This strategy is appropriate only if the dataset is big and numerous values within a tuple are lacking.

Fill the missing values: This assignment can be done in different ways such as: manually completing the missing values using the mean attribute or the most relevant value.

Noisy Data

"Noisy data" is useless data that machines or the machine learning model is unable to interpret. It can be generated as a result of defective data collection or mistakes in data entry, among others. It can be addressed using the methods below:

Binning Method: This technique operates on sorted data to smoothen it out. The entire data set is split into equivalent size sections and then different techniques are used to finish the job. Each section is fixed individually. To fix the entire data set in ago, all data points in a section can be substituted with its "mean" or most probable values.

Regression: In this case, data can be smoothed out by fitting into a "regression function", which can be either "linear" (with one autonomous variable) or "multiple" (with various autonomous variables).

Clustering: This technique is used to group comparable data points into a cluster. The outliers could be obtained with data points falling outside of the clusters or could not be detected.

Data Transformation

This technique is used to convert the data into a format which is suitable for the data mining method. This includes the following ways:

Normalization: This technique is used to scale data values within a defined range, for example, "-1.0 to 1.0" or "0.0 to 1.0".

Attribute Selection: New data attributes can be generated from an existing data set of characteristics, using this technique to assist in the data mining process.

Discretization: This technique is used to "replace raw values of numerical attributes with interval or conceptual levels".

Generation of the concept of hierarchy: This technique is used to transform lower-level data attributes to higher level in the hierarchical setup. For example, you can convert the attribute "city" to "country."

Data Reduction

"Data mining" is a method used for analysis and extraction of insights from Big data. In such instances, analysis becomes more and more difficult to work with given the enormity of data. We use data reduction method to reduce the volume of data set to an optimal and manageable volume. With this method, the cost of data storage and analysis can be significantly lowered while improving the effectiveness of the data storage. It can be dealt with in different respects such as:

Data Cube Aggregation: This technique is used to apply "aggregation operation" to data to effectively build data cubes.

Selection of attribute subset: This technique is used to ensure that only necessary data attributes are used and the not so relevant attributes can be discarded. To perform attribute selection, the "level of significance" and "p-value of the attribute" can be leveraged. The attribute with "p-value" higher than the "significance level" can be removed to obtain the optimal volume of the data set.

Numerosity Reduction: This technique allows the data model to be stored instead of the whole data set or raw data collected from various input sources, for instance, "Regression Models".

Dimensionality Reduction: This technique uses encoding mechanisms to reduce the volume of the data set. If initial data set can be recovered after reconstruction from compressed data set, this reduction in dimensions of the data set is known as "lossless reduction", otherwise it is referred to as "loss reduction". The two efficient techniques of reducing data set "dimensionality" are: "Wavelet transforms" and "PCA (Principal Component Analysis)".

Chapter 9: What Is Unsupervised Machine Learning

We already spent some time looking at the basics of supervised machine learning and some of the different learning algorithms that you are able to work with that fit into this category. Now, it is time to move on to the second type known as unsupervised machine learning.

While supervised machine learning is used in a lot of the different programs that you would like to work with, there are times when it is not going to be the best, or it will end up being too much work to accomplish. This is when you are going to want to start working with unsupervised machine learning.

Unsupervised machine learning is a type of learning that can happen when the chosen learning algorithm is either going to learn from examples or from mistakes, without having the programmer giving it an associated response ahead of time. What this means is that in these kinds of algorithms, the task is going to be in charge of figuring out and analyzing all of the different patterns found in the data based on whatever kind of input is given to it.

The neat thing here is that there are a lot of different types of algorithms that will fit into this kind of category, though we only have time to talk about the top three right now. No matter which of the learning algorithms we choose to go with, you will find that they are effective at taking the data and changing it up so that the data is able to fall into some classes. Many times, this is a useful thing because you will then look all through that information at a later time easier.

There are a lot of times when a programmer will favor the unsupervised machine learning algorithms because these can do a lot of the work that they want, and you are more likely to find these in some programs like the search engine and speech recognition that we talked about before. Unsupervised machine learning is able to set things up so that the computer learns how to do the majority of the work without a human having to write out the instructions or teach it all of the examples.

A good example of how this kind of learning algorithm is going to work is if you have decided it is time to bring out a ton of data and you want to read through it. The point of reading through all of this data is so that you can learn something from it and then make some accurate predictions. This takes too long for most people to do, but the right machine learning algorithm will be able to do it for you. You will also find that the accurate results that you want with a search engine will rely on unsupervised machine learning as well.

There are a number of learning algorithms that are going to fall under the category of unsupervised machine learning. The three types that we are going to explore in this guidebook will include:

1. Neural networks
2. Markov algorithm
3. Clustering algorithms

Working With the Clustering Algorithm

There are a lot of different types of unsupervised machine learning algorithms that you are able to work with in order to see the best results for predictions and more with your project or program. The first option that we are going to take a look at is going to seem pretty simple, but it is definitely one of the best ones for you to choose because of all the information that it will show to you.

The first type of machine learning that we will look at is called the clustering algorithm. With the clustering algorithm, we are going to keep it pretty simple. This method is able to take our data and then classify it into clusters. Before the program even starts, you get the benefit of picking out how many clusters you would like all the information to fit into. For example, you may decide that you want to combine the data into five different clusters. The program would then go through and divide up all the information that you have into five different clusters so that you could look through it.

The nice thing about this algorithm is that it is responsible for doing most of the work for you. This is because it is in charge of how many of your data points are going to fit into those clusters that you chose. To keep things organized, we are going to call all of the main clusters that you picked cluster centroids.

So, when you are looking at one of your clusters and you notice that there are a lot of points inside of it, you can safely make the assumption that all those particular data points have something in common or they are similar. There is some attribute or another that all the data points in one cluster have in common with each other.

Once these original clusters are formed, you can take each of the individual ones and divide them up to get more cluster sets if you would like. You can do this several times, creating more divisions as you go through the steps. In fact, you could potentially go through this enough times that the centroids will stop changing. This is when you know you are done with the process.

There are several reasons why you would want to work with a clustering algorithm to help you get a program started when doing machine learning. First, doing your computations with the help of a clustering algorithm can be easy and cost-efficient, especially compared to some of the supervised learning options that we talked about before. If you would like to do a classification problem, the clustering algorithms are efficient at getting it done.

With that said, you do need to use some caution here though. This algorithm is not going to be able to do the work of showing predictions for you. If you end up with centroids that are not categorized the right way, then you may end up with a project that is done the wrong way.

What is the Markov Algorithm?

Another type of unsupervised machine learning technique that you will want to use here is known as the Markov algorithm. This is the algorithm that you will use when you want it to be able to collect up all of the data given to it or to the system, and then you want the system to be able to translate it. You also want it to take that translated information and put it to work with an additional programming language along the way.

As the programmer, you get a lot of freedom with this one because you are able to go through ahead of time and set up any of the rules that are needed to make this happen. It is useful in other ways as well. For example, you may want to use it to take on a string of data and turn it into something that is useful based on the parameters that you set about how you want the information to behave.

There are many ways that you are able to bring out the Markov algorithm and use it for your needs. One good option to show the power that comes with this is if you want to gather out information that comes with DNA. You would be able to grab a sequence of DNA and then use this kind of learning algorithm in order to take that information and translate it into some numerical values.

As you can imagine here, it is a lot easier for you to go on the computer and read out some values that are numerical, rather than trying to actually read through the strand of DNA that you have. This makes it a lot easier for you to work with that information and see if there are any changes or abnormalities that show up.

Many programmers like to work with this because it is able to take care of any kind of problem where you already know what input you want to be explored, but you aren't quite sure about the exact parameters that you would like to use. This particular learning algorithm is going to look for any information or insights that you can find in that input of information, helping you to learn a lot more than you could on your own.

Even with all of the benefits and different uses that come with the Markov algorithm, there are still going to be some negatives that you should be aware of. Many beginners find that this is a difficult algorithm to work with simply because you must manually search through and make a new rule if you want to use more than one coding language or you want to use a new language.

For those who are using this learning algorithm and who just want to start with one coding language and stick with it, then this isn't something to really worry about since you will just do it once. But there are times when you will work on a program or another thing on the computer and many coding languages will be needed. If this happens for you, then it means that it is required for you to write in new rules each time you change, and this is a long and tedious process to work with.

Chapter 10: Networking

Python is going to provide us with two levels of access to the network services that it has. When you look at the first one, which is known as the low level, you are able to access the basic of the socket support with the help of the operating system on the computer. This is going to be helpful because it allows the programmer to implement clients and servers whether they are working with protocols that are connection-oriented and those that do not have this connection present.

In addition to this low-level option, Python is also going to have some libraries that are considered higher in level. These are going to allow the programmer to have some access to specific application-level network protocols including HTTP and FTP low-level to name a few. In this chapter, we are going to take some of these ideas and explore some of the ways that you are working with Networking Socket Programming.

With this in mind, we need to first take a look at what the sockets are all about and why they will be so important when you work with the idea of networking in Python. Sockets are going to be the endpoints that come with a communication channel that goes bi-directionally. This means that both sides are able to send and receive messages, rather than one side or another being able to only send and the other only being able to receive. Sockets are able to communicate either within the same process, between the processes that happen on the same machine, and even between processes that happen far apart from each other, such as on different continents.

Sockets are going to be interesting and can be helpful with this networking between several processes, and even several different types of machines that you want to work with. You are also able to work with these over a few different types of channels. Some of the examples that you get with this can include UDP, TCP, and the Unix domain. The socket library that you are able to use with the help of Python is going to provide you with a few classes that are designed to handle some of the common transports, along with the generic interface that you can work with and change around in order to handle the rest of the stuff you would like to do.

The neat thing about these sockets is that they are going to have some of their own vocabularies to work with. Knowing some of these terms will make a big difference in how well you are able to work with the sockets, and what you are able to do. Some of the terms that can be helpful when you are working on these sockets and can ensure that your networking with Python will work the way that you want includes

Domain: This is going to be a family of protocols that are used in order to transport the mechanism.

Type: The type of communication that will occur between the two endpoints, usually it is going to be SOCK_STREAM for connection-oriented protocols, and then for the connectionless protocols, you would use SOCK_DGRAM.

Protocol: This is often going to be zero and it is used in a manner to identify the variant of a protocol within the type and the domain that you are working with.

Hostname: This is going to be the identifier that you are going to use with the network interface. Some of the things that we need to know when it comes to the hostname includes:

A string, which can be a hostname, an IPV6 address in a colon notation, a dotted-quad address, or a hostname depending on how it is going to be used in your code.

A string "broadcast" is going to tell us what address we are supposed to send the information out to.

A zero-length string, which is going to specify the INADDR_ANY

An integer, which is going to be interpreted as a binary address in host byte order.

Port: And we need to take a look at the term of the port. Each server is going to be set up to listen for the clients calling on at least one port, but sometimes more. A port can be a Fixnum port number, the name of the service, or some other string that will contain the port number inside.

Now, we need to take a look at the socket module and how we are able to create one of these on our own. To create one of these sockets, we need to work with the function of socket.socket(). You will be able to find this inside the socket module, but the syntax that you are going to need to use in order to make this happen includes:

S = socket.socket (socket_family, socket_type, protocol = 0))

At this point, we need to be able to spend some time looking at the parameters and exploring some of the parameters that are going to come with this one. Some of the descriptions of the parameters that we are able to work with will include the following:

Socket_family. This one is going to come in as either AF_INET or _AF_UNIX.

Socket_type – This is going to come in with the parameters of SOCK_DGRAM or SOCK_STREAM.

Protocol: This one is usually going to be the parameter that is left out, and it is going to default to the 0.

Once you have been able to look through the socket object, then you need to make sure that you are using the functions that are required. These functions need to be in place to make sure that either the server or the client program is set up. The functions that you need to make sure that you are including in this kind of module is going to include some of the following for the server:

S.bind(): This method is going to make sure that the address, which will include the port number pair and the hostname, over to your chosen socket.

S.listen(): This method is going to help us to set up and then start the listener of TCP.

S.accept(). This is going to passively accept the TCP client connection and will also wait until the connection arrives, which is known as blocking.

Then we have a few methods that we are able to use that are going to be considered the client socket methods. Some of the different methods that you can use that will work with the client socket methods rather than the server socket methods include:

1. S.connect()> This is going to be the method that is used in order to actively initiate the TCP server connection that we want to use.

Now that we know a bit about the different socket methods that work with both the server and the client parts of the network, it is time to take a look at a few of the general socket methods that can work with both of these. These are going to be pretty simple to work with and can work with both sides based on whether the endpoint is going to accept or send out the message. The different general socket methods that you can choose to use when doing the Python networking will include:

S.recv(): This is the method that is going to help receive the message of the TCP.

S.send(): This method is going to help to transmit the message with the TCP.

S.recvfrom(): This method is going to help us to receive the message of UDP.

S.sendto(): This method is going to help us to transmit a message that is UDP.

S.close: This is the method that you will use in order to close up the socket that you are working with.

Socket.gethostname): This is the method that is going to help return the hostname back to us.

We have spent quite a bit of time taking a look at some of the things that you can do with this kind of programming and some of the terms that you need to know along the way. With all of this in mind, it is time for us to take a look at some of the codes that we can use to make the networking behave the way that we want to in the process.

The first part we are going to look at is creating our own simple server. To help us write out our own internet servers, we have to make sure to use the socket function, which you will be able to find in the socket module, in order to create a new object of a socket. This kind of socket object is then going to be used in order to call up the other functions to ensure that it sets up the socket server in the process here.

Now, we want to be able to call up the function that is known as the bing(hostname, port) in order to tell the program which port you would like to use for the service on the given host. From there, it is time to call up the method **accept** to deal with the returned object. This method is helpful because it is going to wait until the client will be able to connect themselves to the port that is specified. Once this happens, then it is going to return a connection object, which will then be able to represent the connection that you are able to form with that other client to send messages back and forth.

Chapter 11: Using the Probability And Statistics To Help With Machine Learning

You will find that with machine learning, it is important to recognize that there will be a relationship that will form between this process and the probability theory. Machine learning can be a broad field, and this means that it can intersect with some other fields. The fields that it interacts with will depend on the specific project you will work with. Probability and statistics often merge with machine learning so understanding how these three can work together can be important for your project.

There are a few different ways that statistics and the probability theory will be really important to the whole learning process that goes on with machine learning. First, you have to be able to pick out the right algorithm, and there are quite a few different ones that you can pick from as you will see later on as we progress through this book. The algorithm that you end up picking out needs to have a good balance of things like accuracy, training time, complexity, and a number of parameters. And as you work more with machine learning, you will notice that each project will need a different combination of these factors.

Using the probability theory and statistics, you can better pick out the right parameters for the program, the validation strategies, and make sure that you pick out the right algorithm for your needs. They can be helpful as well for letting you know what level of uncertainty is present inside of your choice so you can guess how much you can trust what is going on.

The probability theory and statistics will help you out quite a bit when it comes to working in machine learning and can help you to understand what is going on with the projects you are working on.

Looking at random variables

Now, the first topic we need to look at when it comes to statistics is random variables. With probability theory, these random variables will be expressed with the "X" symbol, and it is the variable that has all its possible variables come out as numerical outcomes that will come up during one of your random experiments. With random variables, there will be either continuous or discrete options. This means that sometimes your random variables will be functions that will map outcomes to the real value inside their space. We will look at a few examples of this one to help it make sense later on.

We will start out with an example of a random variable by throwing a die. The random variable that we will look at will be represented by X, and it will rely on the outcome that you will get once the die is thrown. The choices of X that would come naturally here will go through to map out the outcome denoted as 1 to the value of i.

What this means is that if X equals 1, you would map the event of throwing a one on your die to being the value of i. You would be able to map this out with any number that is on the die, and it is even possible to take it to the next step and pick out some mappings that are a bit strange. For example, you could map out Y to make it the outcome of 0. This can be a hard process to do, and we aren't going to spend much time on it, but it can help you to see how it works. When we are ready to write out his one, we would have the probability, which is shown as P of outcome 1 of random variable X. it would look like the following:

$PX(i)$ or $(x=i)$

Distribution

Now we need to look at what the probability distribution is like with this process. What we mean here is that we will look at see what the probability of each outcome will be for the random variable. Or, to make it simple, we will see how likely it is that we will get a specific number, like a six or a three, when we throw the die.

To get started with this, we will need to look at an example. We will let the X, or the random variable, be our outcome that we get once the diet is thrown. We will also start with the assumption that the die is not loaded so that all six sides will have the same probability of showing up each time that you throw the diet. The probability distribution for throwing your die and getting a specific number includes:

$PX(1) = PX(2) = \ldots = PX(6) = 1/6$

In this example, it matches up to the what we did with the random variables, it does have a different type of meaning. Your probability distribution is more about the spectrum of events that can happen, while our random variable example is all about which variables are there. With the probability theory, the P(X) part will note that we are working with our probability distribution of the random variable X.

While looking through these examples, you can notice that your distribution will sometimes include two or more variables at the same time. When this happens, we will call it a joint distribution. Your probability will now be determined by each of the variables if there are more than one, that is now involved.

To see how this process will work, let's say that the X is random and that it is defined by what outcome you get when you throw the die, and the Y will be a random variable that will tell you what results that you get when you flip a coin. We will assign a 1 to this coin toss if we get heads at the end, and a 0 will show up if you get tails. This makes it easier when we figure out what the probability distribution is for both of these variables.

Independence

Another variable that you can work with when doing machine learning is to figure out how much independence the problem has. When you are doing random variables, you will find that they will end up being independent of what the other random variables are as long as the variable distribution doesn't change when a new variable is introduced to the equation.

You can make some assumptions about your data in machine learning to help make things easier when you already know about the independence. An example of this is the training sample of "j and i" will be independent of any underlying space when the label of sample "i" is unaffected by the features sample "j". No matter what one of the variables turns out, the other one is not going to be affected by that.

Think back to the example of the die and the coin flip. It doesn't matter what number shows up on the die. The coin will have its own result. And the same can be said the other way around as well. The X random variable is always going to be independent of the Y variable. It doesn't matter the value of Y, but the following code needs to be true for it:

$P(X) = P(X|Y)$.

In the case above, the values that come up for X and for Y variables are dropped because, at this point, the values of these variables are not going to matter that much. But with the statement above, it is true for any type of value that you provide to your X or Y, so it isn't going to matter what values are placed in this equation.

Chapter 12: Data Scrubbing And Preparation

Before you build a machine learning model, you should collect the data and prepare it to ensure that it can be used to train the machine. This is not enjoyable work, but it is essential that you do this so your model is accurate. Engineers often spend hours writing code before they realize that there is something amiss with the data. It is for this reason that experts mention that it is important to clean and scrub the data before it is used to train a model.

Many companies have teams dedicated to cleaning the data that they have collected, but there are many companies that do not worry about this. It is for this reason that most analyses performed using unclean data do not provide accurate results. The goal of any engineer should first be to clean the data, or at least try to clean it to the best of their ability.

Quickly Check Your Data

When you obtain any data set, new or old, you should always verify the contents in that data set using the .head() method.

```
import pandas as pd
df = pd.read_csv('path_to_data')
df.head(10)
>>
```

You will receive some output when you run the above code. This will help you ensure that the data has been picked up from the correct file. You should now look at the types and names of the different columns in the data set. More often than not you will receive data that is not exactly what you are looking for like dates, strings, and other incomprehensible information. Therefore, it is important that you look for these oddities in the beginning.

```
#Get column names
column_names = df.columns
print(column_names)
#Get column data types
df.dtypes
```

#Also check if the column is unique

for i in column_names:

print('{} is unique: {}'.format(i, df[i].is_unique))

You should now look for the index that is associated with the data frame. You can do this by calling on the function called '.index.' You will receive the following error if there is no index attached to the data frame: AttributeError: 'function' object has no attribute 'index.'

#Check the index values

df.index.values

#Check if a certain index exists

'foo' in df.index.values

#If index does not exist

df.set_index('column_name_to_use', inplace=True)

You have now checked most of the data, and are aware of the data types. You will also know if there are any duplicates in the columns in the data set and whether an index has been assigned to the data frame. The next step is to identify the columns that you want to include in your analysis and the columns that you want to get rid of. In the example below we are trying to get rid of the columns that have the indices 1, 3, and 5. For this purpose, we will add the string values to the list which will help us drop the columns.

#Create list comprehension of the columns you want to lose

columns_to_drop = [column_names[i] for i in [1, 3, 5]]

#Drop unwanted columns

df.drop(columns_to_drop, inplace=True, axis=1)

The statement inplace=True has been included in the code to save the file faster. This means that you do not need to save the updated file again. Since most functions and packages in pandas allow you to use the inplace=True statement, you should make the most out of it.

What To Do With NaN?

If you want to identify a way to fill in the blank data or remove any errors in the data set, you should use the two methods dropna() and fillna(). The process of filling blank data and getting rid of errors becomes faster when you use these two methods. That being said, you must ensure that you document every step that you perform so another user can easily understand what it is that you are trying to achieve by writing the code.

You can fill the NaN values with the mean or median value of all the numbers or with strings depending on the data type. Many engineers are still unsure of what they can do with malformed or missing data. This is because the engineer must decide what to do with the data set depending on the type of analysis that he or she is performing.

Experts suggest that engineers use their best judgment or speak to the people they are working with to decide on whether they should remove blank data or fill it using a default value.

```
#Fill NaN with ' '
df['col'] = df['col'].fillna(' ')
#Fill NaN with 99
df['col'] = df['col'].fillna(99)
#Fill NaN with the mean of the column
df['col'] = df['col'].fillna(df['col'].mean())
```

Alternatively, you can choose to move the non-null values backward or forward by using the following statement: method ='pad.' This statement is used as an argument for a method. This argument can be used to fill in values in blank cells or data spaces with the preceding information. You can choose to fill one empty cell or many empty cells by defining the limit. Regardless of what you are doing, ensure that you fill in the information correctly.

```
df = pd.DataFrame(data={'col1':[np.nan, np.nan, 2,3,4, np.nan, np.nan]})
   col1
0  NaN
1  NaN
2  2.0
3  3.0
4  4.0 #This is the value to fill forward
5  NaN
6  NaN
df.fillna(method='pad', limit=1)
   col1
0  NaN
```

1 NaN
2 2.0
3 3.0
4 4.0
5 4.0 #Filled forward
6 NaN

If you look at the above code and the output, you will notice that the data was only filled in the data frame where the index was 5. If there was no limit placed on 'pad,' the full data frame would have been filled. Not only are we limiting forward filling, but we are also using the method bfill to limit backward filling.

#Fill the first two NaN values with the first available value
df.fillna(method='bfill')
    col1
0 2.0 #Filled
1 2.0 #Filled
2 2.0
3 3.0
4 4.0
5 NaN
6 NaN

You can also choose to drop those values from the data frame looking at their rows or columns.

#Drop any rows which have any nans
df.dropna()
#Drop columns that have any nans
df.dropna(axis=1)
#Only drop columns which have at least 90% non-NaNs
df.dropna(thresh=int(df.shape[0] * .9), axis=1)

Alternatively, you can choose to drop a column depending on the number of non-null variables present in a column. You can do this by using the parameter thresh=N.

Dedupe

Dedupe is a library which uses machine learning to identify duplicates in a data set. We will be using the Chicago Early Childhood Location data set for the examples in this section.
#Columns and the number of missing values in each
Id has 0 na values
Source has 0 na values
Site name has 0 na values
Address has 0 na values
Zip has 1333 na values
Phone has 146 na values
Fax has 3299 na values
Program Name has 2009 na values
Length of Day has 2009 na values
IDHS Provider ID has 3298 na values
Agency has 3325 na values
Neighborhood has 2754 na values
Funded Enrollment has 2424 na values
Program Option has 2800 na values
Number per Site EHS has 3319 na values
Number per Site HS has 3319 na values
Director has 3337 na values
Head Start Fund has 3337 na values
Early Head Start Fund has 2881 na values
CC fund has 2818 na values
Progmod has 2818 na values
Website has 2815 na values
Executive Director has 3114 na values
Center Director has 2874 na values
ECE Available Programs has 2379 na values
NAEYC Valid Until has 2968 na values
NAEYC Program Id has 3337 na values
Email Address has 3203 na values
Ounce of Prevention Description has 3185 na values
Purple binder service type has 3215 na values

Column has 3337 na values

Column2 has 3018 na values

You should save the method as the cleaning package. This will make it easier for you to deal with duplicate data.

```
import pandas as pd
import numpy
import dedupe
import os
import csv
import re
from unidecode import unidecode
def preProcess(column):
    '''
    Used to prevent errors during the dedupe process.
    '''
    try:
        column = column.decode('utf8')
    except AttributeError:
        pass
    column = unidecode(column)
    column = re.sub(' +',' ', column)
    column = re.sub('\n',' ', column)
    column = column.strip().strip('"').strip("'").lower().strip()

    if not column:
        column = None
    return column
```

Let us now begin to import the information in the .csv column by column when we are processing the data.

```
def readData(filename):

    data_d = {}
    with open(filename) as f:
        reader = csv.DictReader(f)
        for row in reader:
```

```
        clean_row = [(k, preProcess(v)) for (k, v) in row.items()]
        row_id = int(row['Id'])
        data_d[row_id] = dict(clean_row)
return df
name_of_file = 'data.csv'
print('Cleaning and importing data ... ')
df = readData(name_of_file)
```

At this point we will need to let the function know the different categories and features it would need to look at before it determines the duplicate values. The features have been denoted by the term fields in the section below, and each of these fields is assigned a data type. The output also mentions if there are any missing values in the data set. There are a list of different types that you are allowed to use here, but let us stick to rows if we want to keep things simple. We will also not look at every column to look for duplicate values. You can, however, do this if you believe it will help your cause.

```
#Set fields
fields = [
        {'field' : 'Source', 'type': 'Set'},
        {'field' : 'Site name', 'type': 'String'},
        {'field' : 'Address', 'type': 'String'},
        {'field' : 'Zip', 'type': 'Exact', 'has missing' : True},
        {'field' : 'Phone', 'type': 'String', 'has missing' : True},
        {'field' : 'Email Address', 'type': 'String', 'has missing' : True},
        ]
```

Let us now begin to feed the package with some information.

```
#Pass in our model
deduper = dedupe.Dedupe(fields)
#Check if it is working
deduper
>>
<dedupe.api.Dedupe at 0x11535bbe0>
#Feed some sample data in ... 15000 records
deduper.sample(df, 15000)
```

Let us now move onto the labelling part. You will prompt the dedupe package to label the data when you run this method.

dedupe.consoleLabel(deduper)

Do these records refer to the same thing?

(y)es / (n)o / (u)nsure / (f)inished

You will no longer need to search or peruse through large volumes of data to see if there is any duplication within the data frame. You can use a neural network to identify the duplicates in the data set. When you provide the network with labeled data, finish training the model, and save the progress, you can be certain that the network predicts the data correctly.

deduper.train()

#Save training

with open(training_file, 'w') as tf:
    deduper.writeTraining(tf)

#Save settings

with open(settings_file, 'wb') as sf:
    deduper.writeSettings(sf)

Now that we are almost done, we will need to identify a way to set a threshold for the data set. When the value of the variable recall_weight is one, we are asking the deduper package to be more precise or recall the value. If the value of recall_weight is greater than one, there will be more than one recall. You can always work with these settings to identify the process that works best for the model you are developing.

threshold = deduper.threshold(df, recall_weight=1)

We can now look through the data frame to identify where the duplicates exist. It is easier to do this using the model instead of doing this by hand.

#Cluster the duplicates together

clustered_dupes = deduper.match(data_d, threshold)

print('There are {} duplicate sets'.format(len(clustered_dupes)))

Let us now look at the duplicates.

clustered_dupes

>>

[((0, 1, 215, 509, 510, 1225, 1226, 1879, 2758, 3255),
   array([0.88552043, 0.88552043, 0.77351897, 0.88552043, 0.88552043,
       0.88552043, 0.88552043, 0.89765924, 0.75684386, 0.83023088])),

((2, 3, 216, 511, 512, 1227, 1228, 2687), ...

This does not actually say much about the data set. So, what do you think this output shows us? What has happened to all the values in the data set? If you pay close attention to these values (0, 1, 215, 509, 510, 1225, 1226, 1879, 2758, 3255), they indicate the locations for where the duplicates are. These locations are the parts where deduper thinks the values are the same. We can always look at the original data if we want to verify this.

{'Id': '215',

'Source': 'cps_early_childhood_portal_scrape.csv',

'Site name': 'salvation army temple',

'Address': '1 n. ogden',

...

{'Id': '509',

'Source': 'cps_early_childhood_portal_scrape.csv',

'Site name': 'salvation army - temple / salvation army',

'Address': '1 n ogden ave',

'Zip': None,

..

This looks like a bunch of duplicates, doesn't it? You can use deduper for many other functions like interaction fields where there is a multiplicative and not additive interaction between the fields or as a matchblock for numerous sequences.

Matching Strings Using Fuzzywuzzy

You should always try to use this library when you are comparing strings. This is because this package gives you a score that will help you understand how similar two strings are. This is a tool that most engineers use since they can use this package to identify any issues with data validation. They can also use this tool to clean the data set or perform any analysis. This approach will only work on small data sets. That being said, you can always use fuzzywuzzy if you want to match strings in a more scientific manner. This package uses the Levenshtein distance when it compares two strings. This distance is calculated as the distance between the similarity metric of two strings. The metric is calculated as the distance between the number of edits that need to be made to characters in order to change one word into another.

For example, if you want to change the string bar into foo or vice versa, you would need to make at least three edits if you want to change one word to another. This is the Levenshtein distance. Let us see how we can do this in practice.

```
$ pip3 install fuzzywuzzy
#test.py
from fuzzywuzzy import fuzz
from fuzzywuzzy import process
foo = 'is this string'
bar = 'like that string?'
fuzz.ratio(foo, bar)
>>
71
fuzz.WRatio(foo, bar) #Weighted ratio
>>
73
fuzz.UQRatio(foo, bar) #Unicode quick ratio
>> 73
```

The fuzzywuzzy package gives you access to different functions that you can use to evaluate the strings in your data set. We will only look at the standard implementation of this logic for the purpose of this book. We will then look at tokenized strings which will return the measure of similarity between the sequences. These tokens will lie within a range of zero and hundred. The token will be sorted before it is used to compare strings. This is important since you not only want to know what the string contains, but also want to know its position.

The strings bar and foo have been allotted the same tokens, but these are different. So, you cannot expect to treat them in the same way. You can therefore look for this difference within your data set and make any adjustments if necessary.

```
foo = 'this is a foo'
bar = 'foo a is this'
fuzz.ratio(foo, bar)
```

\>\>

31

fuzz.token_sort_ratio('this is a foo', 'foo a is this')

\>\>

100

The next best thing you can do is to find the closest match from a list of values. Let us look at an example where we will be looking for Harry Potter titles. Many people do not remember the titles of all the Harry Potter books. So, they can use this method to score the books so that the machine can predict the name of the book. If you were to guess "fire," the machine will score the list and display the title with "fire" in it as the output.

```
lst_to_eval = ['Harry Potter and the Philosopher's Stone',
'Harry Potter and the Chamber of Secrets',
'Harry Potter and the Prisoner of Azkaban',
'Harry Potter and the Goblet of Fire',
'Harry Potter and the Order of the Phoenix',
'Harry Potter and the Half-Blood Prince',
'Harry Potter and the Deathly Hallows']
#Top two responses based on my guess
process.extract("fire", lst_to_eval, limit=2)
```

\>\>

[('Harry Potter and the Goblet of Fire', 60), ("Harry Potter and the Sorcerer's Stone", 30)

```
results = process.extract("fire", lst_to_eval, limit=2)
for result in results:
  print('{}: has a score of {}'.format(result[0], result[1]))
```

\>\>

Harry Potter and the Goblet of Fire: has a score of 60

Harry Potter and the Sorcerer's Stone: has a score of 30

If you want, you can return only one value.

```
>>> process.extractOne("stone", lst_to_eval)
```

("Harry Potter and the Sorcerer's Stone", 90)

Let us now look at a similar application of the fuzzywuzzy package. You can use a list of strings that contain duplicates and use this package to remove those duplicates. This function is not as fancy or amazing as a neural network, but it works perfectly well on small data sets.

Let us continue with the Harry Potter example. We now want to look for duplicate characters in the book using the character list. For this, you must set the threshold between zero and one hundred. Let us make the default 70. Remember that as the threshold decreases the number of duplicates in the data set will increase.

```
#List of duplicate character names
contains_dupes = [
'Harry Potter',
'H. Potter',
'Harry James Potter',
'James Potter',
'Ronald Bilius \'Ron\' Weasley',
'Ron Weasley',
'Ronald Weasley']
#Print the duplicate values
process.dedupe(contains_dupes)
>>
dict_keys(['Harry James Potter', "Ronald Bilius 'Ron' Weasley"])
#Print the duplicate values with a higher threshold
process.dedupe(contains_dupes, threshold=90)
>>
dict_keys(['Harry James Potter', 'H. Potter', "Ronald Bilius 'Ron' Weasley"])
```

You can also perform some fuzzywuzzy matching using the datetime package. This package will allow you to extract different dates from strings. You should use this package when you do not want to make use of the regex expression.

```
from dateutil.parser import parse
dt = parse("Today is January 1, 2047 at 8:21:00AM", fuzzy=True)
print(dt)
>>
2047-01-01 08:21:00
dt = parse("May 18, 2049 something something", fuzzy=True)
```

```
print(dt)
>>
2049-05-18 00:00:00
```

The Concept of Truncation

It represents all possible clusterings, from the finest clustering (one cluster per individual) to the coarser one (a single cluster for all individuals).

The next question may then arise: at which level of aggregation should we "cut" the tree, that is, how to define the most relevant number of clusters? Quantitative responses can be made, based on the relative gain in inertia generated by moving from one partition to another, but remember that visual inspection of the dendrogram often gives very good answers. We can then rely on criteria such as:

- The general shape of the tree: it often reveals a "logical" cutting level indicated by significant jumps in the values of the level indices. If these jumps concern the k last nodes of the tree, then a division into (k + 1) classes will be relevant;

- The number of clusters: avoid too many, in which case clustering loses its interest;

- The ability to interpret clusters: no need to try to retain clusters for which we cannot give business sense; focus on clusters that make sense.

Non-hierarchical clustering

The objective of non-hierarchical clustering is the same as for hierarchical clustering, but this time, we know in advance how many clusters to build. For a given measurement of the distance of individuals and for a number of known classes, one can easily imagine a simple and optimal classification solution: enumerate all possible grouping possibilities and keep the best. However, this solution is not applicable in practice, because the number of combinations of possible groupings becomes very quickly huge. But approximate solutions can be obtained through heuristics, and several algorithms of this kind exist. Their fundamental principle is contained in the method of mobile centers.

Mobile centers

Let's talk now about some of the most popular variants of mobile centers, designed to improve certain aspects.

Some variants

They are numerous, and we will limit ourselves to mentioning four:

- The k-means method: it works exactly like the mobile centers, with one difference, which is the calculation of the centers. A refocusing is done as soon as an individual changes cluster. It is no longer expected that all individuals are assigned to a cluster to calculate the centers of gravity, they are changed as and when reassignments;

- The dynamic cloud method: it favors the search for stable groups. It is a generalization of mobile centers whose idea is to associate with each cluster a representative different from its center of gravity. In the majority of cases, the center of gravity is replaced by a set of individuals, called "stallions" and constituting a "core". This nucleus is supposed to have better descriptive power than point centers. Note that other more exotic representatives can be used: a straight line, a law of probability, etc.;

- The Isodata method: the principle of mobile centers is preserved, but constraints will make it possible to control the development of clustering. These constraints serve to prevent the formation of groups with too small a number or a large diameter;

- The k-medoids method: it is similar to the k-means method, with one difference. Indeed, it will no longer define a class by a mean value (the center of gravity, on centroid), but by its most central representative (the medoid). It is, therefore, an individual from the cluster who will represent the latter. This method has the advantage of being more robust to outliers;

- Self-Organizing Maps: this algorithm differs from mobile centers by updating neighboring clusters, where clusters become activatable neurons. This nonlinear method allows in fine to preserve all the topology of the data, starting more often from a rectangular grid of neurons which will be deformed.

Let's stop there the enumeration of methods with names that are stranges! We recommend that you select a "basic" method, such as a moving center or dynamic cloud, and then move on to more elaborate methods if the results are not satisfactory.

Mixed approaches

By mixing the approaches, we can take advantage of the main advantages of the different methods, namely:

- **The capacity to analyze a large number of individuals, a strong point of non-hierarchical methods (for a number of observations greater than 103, it becomes difficult to apply hierarchical methods directly);**

- **The choice of an optimal number of classes, made possible by the hierarchical classification.**

Introduction to decision trees

In their simple form, they are very rarely used in machine learning. On the other hand, the understanding of their principles and their methods of construction is a prerequisite for the study of the random forest, the first chapter of the part presenting the tools of "heavy artillery" which are at the disposal of the data scientist.

Principle

The general purpose of a decision tree is to explain a value from a series of discrete or continuous variables. We are thus in a very classical case of matrix X with m observations and n variables, associated with a vector Y to explain. The values Y can be of two kinds:

- Continuous: one speaks then of the tree of regression;

- Or qualitative: we will speak of the classification tree.

These inductive methods have many advantages: they are fairly powerful, non-parametric and nonlinear. In principle, they will partition individuals by producing groups of individuals that are as homogeneous as possible from the point of view of the variable to be predicted, taking into account a hierarchy of the predictive capacity of the variables considered. This hierarchy makes it possible to visualize the results in a tree and to constitute explanatory rules explicit, oriented business.

The main rules definition principles are as follows (inspired by Tufféry, 2011). Several iterations are necessary: to each of them, we divide the individuals into k classes (usually k = 2), to explain the output variable. The first division is obtained by choosing the explanatory variable that will provide the best separation of individuals. This division defines sub-populations, represented by the "nodes" of the tree. Each node is associated with a measure of proportion, which makes it possible to explain the membership of a class or the meaning of an output variable. The operation is repeated for each subpopulation until no further separation is possible. We then obtain terminal nodes, called "leaves" of the tree. Each leaf is characterized by a specific path through the tree called a rule. The set of rules for all sheets is the template.

The interpretation of a rule is easy if one obtains pure sheets (for example, 100% of variables to be explained are TRUE or FALSE for a given rule). Otherwise, it is necessary to rely on the empirical distribution of the variable to predict on each node of the tree.

Chapter 13: Tips to Make Machine Learning Work For You

Now that we have spent some time in this guidebook taking a look at machine learning and all of the great learning algorithms that fit into the mix, along with the different categories that come with supervised, unsupervised, and reinforcement learning, it is time to move on to actually putting these to use. There are so many different situations where you are able to utilize what you know from machine learning, and it is going to really make a difference if you are able to work on these algorithms.

Once you have a good idea with these algorithms, you may be more curious about some of the tips and strategies that you are able to use in order to make sure that machine learning is going to work out the way that you would like. Some of the tips that you can follow when it comes to working with machine learning include:

Remember the Logistics

When you are working on machine learning, remember that success is not always just about picking out the right kind of algorithm or tool. In fact, it takes a bit more for this. You need to find a good fit and a good design for the specific kind of problem or project that you want to work with. Each project is going to be different and if you try to use the same things for each one, then there are going to be situations where machine learning will not be successful.

For example, the machine learning that you use with a campaign for online marketing is going to be a lot different compared to working with an algorithm that helps guide an autonomous car. Expanding your resources for an incremental algorithm improvement is going to be really worth it when it comes to the car, but in most marketing cases, you would want to optimize the different logistics around you instead.

This means that before you even get started on the project that you would like to use, you need to take some time to figure out the kind of logistics that are going to make the most sense for what you want to do. We talked about a lot of different algorithms that we can use based on the kind of project or program that you would like to focus on. And each of them presented us with something that was a bit different. Learning how to make these work and picking the right one for the job is important to getting the results that you want.

Mind the Data

Another option that we need to pay attention to is the data that you are going to put through the algorithm. One of the biggest considerations to making sure that all the algorithms you use deliver insights that are valuable is that you have to feed it the right kind of data. If you find that you are running data through an algorithm and the results are not coming out the way that you think they should, then it is most likely the data you are using is not right, rather than the algorithm.

There are a lot of programmers or business owners who are going to get all ego-bound and wound up, being stuck to one particular algorithm. But with all of the different tools out there, there is the possibility for way too many new algorithms. While choosing the right algorithm is indeed important to the whole process, the thing that is even more important here is making sure that you are choosing the right kind of data to help you out.

If you are studying with a harder or more complex problem like speech recognition or even something like computer vision, then that is one thing. But this field, despite what we may think when we get a bit lost in it, is that we are in a field that is data-driven. In most of the scenarios that we are going to find ourselves in, making some adjustments to the data that we put in rather than the algorithm is going to make a difference.

Any time that the algorithm is not providing you with the results that make sense or the results that you should be getting when you give it a try, then it is time to make some changes. Maybe you are putting in too much data, or the wrong kind of data, or even not enough data. Changing things around a bit and seeing what that does to the predictions you get may be just the change that you are looking for.

Algorithms Are Not Always Right

We spent a lot of time in this guidebook taking a look at the various algorithms that you are able to focus on. These are great tools that are going to help you to get the right results that you want, but they are not always right. If we start to look at them as magic bullets that are going to solve all of our problems instantly, then this could be a bad thing.

Implementations of machine learning are going to do their very best when there is a continual process of trial and error. No matter how good you may think the algorithms you use are if the system is doing any kind of interaction with another person, or more than one people, then it has to have some adjustments done to it over time. Businesses need to always be measuring the effectiveness of their implementation and figure out if there are any variables and changes that are going to either make it better or make it worse.

This is going to sound like a lot of work and may seem a bit confusing when you are first getting into the field of machine learning. But it is something that you need to focus on. Very few businesses are doing this. Instead, they assume that their algorithm is perfect and that it never needs to be changed. This is going to make things worse, and over time, the algorithm is going to be so far behind that it is not going to be able to give you accurate results.

It is normal to want to deploy your system with an algorithm and then want it to do its job perfectly, without ever having to do any work to keep it that way. While that would be the ideal world, that is not a reality that any of us can count on. No algorithm or user interface design is going to be able to stick around for a long time to come. And there is no data collection method that is going to be superseded.

That means that no matter what kind of algorithm you decide to go with, it is going to need some tune-ups and adjustments over time. If you keep up with this and don't let it fall to the side, then it is likely that the adjustments are going to be small and won't require a ton of work on your part to complete. The biggest issues are going to come when you start to ignore this step, and then the issues start to compound on each other. Remember that no algorithm, no matter how great it may seem, is going to be perfect and you do need to check on it on occasion.

Pick out a toolset that is diverse

As you can imagine from this guidebook and some of the other research that you may have done with machine learning, there are many different tools available to you with this field, and many of them are going to be available to you for free! This is a great thing because it allows you to have access to countless different resources available to help you get started.

But with this in mind, don't let yourself get glued to one tool. You may have one that is your favorite and that you want to use all of the time. But in reality, when you are working with machine learning, you will really need to bring out several to make this successful. If there is someone around who is trying to convince you that one tool is the only one that is going to work and that you don't need any of the others, then it is time to move away from them and learn about all of the other tools that are really out there.

The neat thing about machine learning is that it is growing like crazy and there are so many people who are interested in learning more about it and using it for their own needs. This is good news for you because there are going to be a lot of different tools available. Experiment a few and figure out which ones are the best for you. And consider the fact that you are going to need to use a few of these in order to help you to get the work done.

Try Out Some Hybrid Learning

Another thing that you can work with is the idea of hybrid learning. You are able to mix together some deep learning with some cheap learning to come up with a hybrid. One example of this is that you are able to take a vision model on a computer that is already in existence and then re-construct the top few layers, the layers that are going to contain the decision that you want to be made. From there, you are able to co-opt a framework that is existing, and then use it for a new case.

This is a great way for you to really make something new, without having to create the whole thing from the very beginning. You are able to use some of the techniques and frameworks that are already in existence, and then add some of the specifications and more that are present in it to get the results that you would like.

This can take a bit of work. But think through some of the projects that you want to work with. Break it up into some smaller parts and figure out whether there are any existing platforms or frameworks that you are able to use to get things started. Once you have this, you will be able to go through and make the changes that are needed, perhaps using some of the algorithms that we already have in place and talked about above, to make this happen.

This is a benefit in many ways. First, the frameworks that you are going to be using are free in most cases or at least are not going to cost you all that much. This means that you will be able to use them and save money compared to recreating exactly what you want from scratch. It is always a good thing in business when you are able to save money. You still get to use the deep learning that is needed in the process, but you get the benefit of saving money on the parts that don't necessarily need to be unique.

Another benefit here is that you can save yourself some time. Many of the frameworks that you are going to use take a lot of time to create. And if you have to come up with a new one each time that you start, it is going to take forever to get projects done. When you are able to use or purchase the one that you would like, you can end up saving a lot of time and it speeds along with the project that you want to get done.

Chapter 14: Strengths of AI Science

One of the overarching benefits of AI is that consumers and businesses both stand to benefit from improvements in existing artificial intelligence technology. Technology can be leveraged to improve customer outcomes and to make providers more efficient, especially in healthcare. Many aspects of healthcare poise this industry to be impacted dramatically by AI advancements. In the healthcare industry, time and access are often factors that can impact the ability of providers to engage care.

For example, if a patient has suffered a certain type of stroke, they need to be evaluated by a provider and seen at a high-level medical center within a certain window in order to receive certain medication. Ways that AI can improve the ability of providers to give care in this type of scenario includes by providing the doctor and team with relevant patient information before the patient reaches the center, and by performing analysis of patient data that assists the provider in making the diagnosis.

This type of AI capability would fall under the term deep learning because it would require that AI agents be trained using training data to help them to learn how to distinguish patients of one type from patients of another type. This ability of AI to categorize data using unsupervised or semi-supervised learning is an important dimension in AI research because it allows AI to learn patterns in a similar way that human beings do (or even better). Present day limitations of this type of learning include the reality that AI does not always apply what it has learned in previous experiences to new experiences, so this type of application in healthcare would need to be supervised by healthcare staff before AI can be allowed to act with relative independence.

AI is also changing business and marketing in compelling ways. Because AI is able to analyze data quickly, efficiently, and often uniquely, machine learning tools can provide businesses with predictive analyses that can guide business decisions and increase competitive advantage. Indeed, much of the power of AI in business is not in the AI tools that AI markets to consumers, but in the behind the scenes work that machine learning does in helping businesses change their practices in powerful ways.

AI advancements in these areas can potentially save businesses billions and increase profits, so it may be wise for business leaders and even lay people to pay attention here.

AI Taking the Lead in Healthcare

Healthcare is an industry being pulled in two different directions. On the one hand, technological advancements are necessary to reduce mortality rates, improve patient outcomes, and reduce healthcare costs, but there is also a concern that healthcare may become dehumanized because of increased reliance on technology. Indeed, even video conferencing utilities in healthcare have been met with controversy in some quarters because it takes away that hands-on care that is so essential in medicine.

In this section, we will examine some of the ways that artificial intelligence is changing healthcare. Below is a list of some of the main areas:

- Using IoT to provide diagnostic information, i.e., smartphone images and video
- Healthcare monitoring using heart rate monitors and other wearable devices
- Analysis of the electronic medical record for predictive analytics
- Developing new medicines using machine learning
- Medical image analysis in pathology and radiology
- Analysis of the electronic medical record for resistant antibiotic risk
- Language processing in dictation of medical records
- Improving healthcare access by providing automated services in underserved areas
- Using brain-computer interfaces to improve quality of life in stroke and other trauma to the nervous system

We have already explored the idea of image analysis converging with machine learning and IoT to provide doctors with diagnostic information. This idea has been controversial because it takes away some of the diagnostic tasks away from the physician and gives it to the AI agent, but unfortunately, this may be necessary in certain cases. For example, a patient suffering trauma who is far from a trauma center may benefit from this type of analysis before the patient completes the long journey to the hospital. This type of activity has already begun to be used in some parts of Asia and is usually involves using a smartphone to take an image of some kind or record a video and this patient data being uploaded to a cloud-based platform.

This type of application for AI in healthcare has also been suggested for use in countries like the United States, especially in underserved communities. There is a shortage of qualified healthcare providers in many of these communities and the idea here is that AI could either take over some duties of triage or at least could aid providers that have large patient lists and are short in time. This, of course, is a controversial area as it implies that low-income groups should have their care handled by AI rather than by more expensive human beings, although it is likely that countries like the US will see some developments in this area.

AI Making Great Change in Business and Marketing

AI has already begun to revolutionize business and marketing. Predictive analytics is a term that has cropped up several times in this book. It is one of the major uses of AI in business and marketing, but it is not the only one. The advantages of predictive analytics in marketing are clear. This type of AI functionality can use data to predict customer behavior for decision making, or it can recommend products to customers and market them appropriately. Below is a list of some other ways in which AI technology is changing this particular field:

- Creation of unique content (copywriting)
- Creation of sales forecasts
- Speech recognition in voice-activated devices
- Conversational AI and chatbots
- Augmented reality and computer vision

- Ad targeting as part of programmatic advertising
- High-precision product pricing
- Dynamic segmentation and audience targeting
- Sentiment analysis
- Image recognition and visual search
- Product recommendations

The list of potential AI uses is a long one, and the list above represents solely some of the main areas. Indeed, there is some overlap in the areas where AI can be used in marketing. For example, voice recognition can be a part of several different AI applications, as can image recognition and predictive analytics. Some examples of how business leaders might easily apply these applications include creating a chatbot on their website that allows customers to ask questions and have them answered appropriately, and incorporating AI into company websites to allow for product recommendations as well as provide predictive analytical data back to company decision makers.

This last point is important to stress when it comes to AI applications in general, not just AI in business and marketing. Big tech companies, as we have seen, have been so successful with AI not only because they have lots of data and have been willing to experiment with this technology, but because they have machine learning teams and data science departments that oversee AI, analyze data, and provide input to leadership for decision-making purposes. Using AI at the present time does not mean simply shoving an application into your website or server, it also means having information channels where relevant persons can exchange information and make company decisions based on input gained from AI.

Conclusion

Thank you for making it through to the end of this book. Let's hope it was informative and able to provide you with all of the tools you need to achieve your goals whatever they may be.

The next step is to take a look at the different types of machine learning, and then decide which one is going to work the best for your needs. There are so many different aspects that come with machine learning, and we sincerely hope that you were able to find the information that you need to help you get started with this kind of programming.

You will find that working with machine learning is going to be a bit different than what you did with the traditional coding languages that you may have worked with in the past. This is what makes it more entertaining and fun, and it certainly doesn't mean that the process is going to be more difficult. You will be amazed at all of the complex tasks that you are able to work on, with the simplicity of machine learning.

When you are ready to work on some of your own codes with machine learning, and you want to be able to do it with some confidence that the programs are going to be great, make sure to check out this guidebook to help you get started.

www.ingramcontent.com/pod-product-compliance
Lightning Source LLC
Chambersburg PA
CBHW070847070326
40690CB00009B/1738